BLUES LICK FACTORY
BUILDING GREAT BLUES RIFFS

By Jesse Gress

Backbeat
Books

An Imprint of Hal Leonard Corporation
New York

Book layout by Stephen Ramirez

Library of Congress Cataloging-in-Publication Data is available upon request.
ISBN 10: 0-87930-913-X
ISBN 13: 978-0-87930-913-8

Published in 2007 by
Backbeat Books (an imprint of Hal Leonard Corporation)
19 West 21st Street
New York, NY 10010

Printed in the United States of America

www.backbeatbooks.com

BLUES LICK FACTORY

TABLE OF CONTENTS

BLUES LICK FACTORY

ACKNOWLEDGMENTS

In loving memory of Dr. Francis A. Gress, a father, teacher, humanitarian, and healer of the highest order.

Deepest thanks and love to Mary Lou and Deidre, my extended Gress, Tresolini, and Arnold families, early blues mentors the Nastasee Brothers and Brad Steckel, and to Todd Rundgren and Tony Levin for taking me around the world and allowing me to smear my blues all over their strange and beautiful music.

A heapin' helpin' of gratitude goes to the usual suspects at Backbeat Books—Richard Johnston, Nina Lesowitz, Kevin Becketti, Gail Saari, and Dorothy Cox, plus a special thanks to Matt Kelsey for getting the ball rolling—and to Clare Cerullo, Gail Siragusa, Claudine Krystyniak, Carol Flannery, and John Cerullo at Hal Leonard.

KEY TO NOTATIONAL SYMBOLS

The following symbols are used in *Blues Lick Factory* to notate fingerings, techniques, and effects commonly used in guitar music. Certain symbols are found in either the tablature or the standard notation only, not both. For clarity, consult both systems.

HOW TABLATURE WORKS

The horizontal lines represent the guitar's strings, the top line standing for the high *E*. The numbers designate the frets to be played. For instance, a 2 positioned on the first line would mean play the 2nd fret on the first string (0 indicates an open string). Time values are indicated on the standard notation staff seen directly above the tablature. Special symbols and instructions appear between the standard and tablature staves. Fret-hand fingering is designated by small Arabic numerals below the tablature staff (1=first finger, 2=middle finger, 3=third finger, 4=little finger, t=thumb).

⊓ : **Pick downstroke.**

V : **Pick upstroke.**

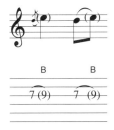

Bend: Play the first note and bend to the pitch of the equivalent fret position shown in parentheses. Notes can also be pre-bent.

Reverse Bend: Bend the note to the specified pitch/fret position shown in parentheses, then release to the indicated pitch/fret.

Hammer-on: From lower to higher note(s). Individual notes may also be hammered.

Pull-off: From higher to lower note(s).

Slide: Play first note and slide up or down to the next pitch. If the notes are tied, pick only the first. If no tie is present, pick both.

A slide symbol before or after a single note indicates a slide to or from an undetermined pitch.

Finger vibrato.

Bar dips.

CHORD DIAGRAMS

In all chord diagrams, vertical lines represent the strings, and horizontal lines represent the frets. The following symbols are used:

——	Nut; indicates first position.
X	Muted string, or string not played.
○	Open string.
⌒	Barre (partial or full).
●	Placement of left-hand fingers.
III	Roman numerals indicate the fret at which a chord is located.

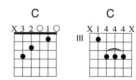

Arabic numerals indicate fret-hand fingering.

HOW TO USE THIS BOOK

Welcome (or, if you are a return customer, welcome back) to the *Blues Lick Factory*. Our new introductory guide to the single-note vocabulary of blues guitar was designed as both a self-contained edition and a companion volume to the blues section of the original *Guitar Lick Factory* and has been expanded with new material and an audio component, the latter a long-standing request from previous clients. You will find that many of our licks and philosophies are common to both facilities. In fact, the first 109 examples in *Blues Lick Factory* correspond to the modular three-, four-, five-, and six-note licks in *Guitar Lick Factory* (except for Examples 27 through 32, which are new additions), but each one has been rechristened as a "pickup lick" and is now applied to various target tones related to the I, IV, and V chords that form a standard 12-bar blues progression. We now offer a number of specific contexts and target options for each lick, while still allowing complete compatibility for experimentation with the phrasing and fingering options demonstrated in the acclaimed multioctave/multifingering grids in *Guitar Lick Factory*.

And that's just the first of many renovations. We also clue you in on valuable production methods for expanding our line of pickup modules into one-bar licks, two-bar-licks, and, ultimately, 12-bar solos. Most important and due to popular demand, we include an audio demonstration of every example. We're not out to break any speed records here (that's up to you), so all of the licks on the accompanying CD are demonstrated at a fairly leisurely pace.

Additionally, *Blues Lick Factory* approaches the manufacturing process in a more methodical manner than our previous facility. Although you certainly can (and presumably will) pursue the subject matter much further, our production line stresses the conversion of raw blues-based materials into a final and useful end product by formulating a beginning, a middle, and an ending to the process. (Wouldn't it feel great to actually *finish* a guitar method book?) You will review the scales and chord progressions that comprise the foundation of the blues vocabulary, explore the concept of target tones, discover tritones and a slew of I-, IV-, and V-chord voicings, learn how to apply more than 100 three-, four-, five-, and six-note pickup modules to five different target tones for each chord, and how to develop single target tones into one-bar licks, then how to combine these into two-bar licks for use in specific parts of a blues progression, and finally, how to construct complete 12-bar blues solos and accompanying rhythm figures—in that order.

Once again, the middle-ground key of *A* provides global compatibility between licks, and 3/8 (for short modules) and 12/8 (for one-bar and longer licks) have been selected as time signatures due to their accuracy in depicting both triplet-based slow blues grooves and medium- to up-tempo shuffles. (Note: In 12/8, a dotted quarter note, which contains three eighth notes, constitutes one beat.) Our four-note pickup licks utilize a 2/4 time signature to provide a model for rhythmic conversion from 3/8, and our "Rhythmic Variations" department allows you to swap out any stock three-, four-, five-, and six-note pickup lick for an optional custom 3/8 or 2/4 rhythm.

As mentioned previously, all of the additional fingering, octave, and especially phrasing options found throughout the original *Guitar Lick Factory*, including bends, hammer-ons, pull-offs, slides, and, of course, a soulful vibrato, which should be honed at every available opportunity, can also be (and, in many cases, have been) applied to the licks presented here. (Sorry, folks. There's simply not enough room to include them in our new digs.) In both books, the emphasis is on creating cohesive, emotive blues lines and solos by stringing together endless variations of short, modular blues licks. Get enough of our three-, four-, five-, and six-note pickup modules under your fingers, learn to string them together and vary their phrasing and rhythm, and you will begin to understand how blues guitarists gain such conversational command of their language.

In keeping with our more-notes-less-talk philosophy, you won't find many flowery metaphors or stylistic comparisons to blues artists referenced in these pages. We simply present one take, in a clear, straightforward, and logical manner, on the nuts-and-bolts blues guitar pedagogy that has been passed between multiple generations and let nature take its course. (Less views = more blues!) Our mission statement is to get these licks off the page and into your psyche so you can become conversant in this universal language as soon as possible. Just follow the guidelines that precede each chapter to get the most out of your tenure at *Blues Lick Factory*, and you will emerge a seasoned pro ready for your next head-cutting session!

CHAPTER 1

BLUES SCALES AND CHORD PROGRESSIONS

Melodically, most blues licks are derived from the pentatonic major, pentatonic minor, and blues scales. Though all of the licks in this book are presented in the key of *A*, they are transposable to any key. Familiarize yourself with these scales and their fretboard patterns in all keys. (Write 'em down!) Once you connect a lick to its host fretboard pattern, you can transpose it to any key by simply moving it up or down the neck to the appropriate position, or by jumping to different octaves and string groups. Figures A through C depict the *A* pentatonic major, pentatonic minor, and blues scales on full fretboard grids and broken into five connected "box" patterns:

Figure A

A Pentatonic Major Scale

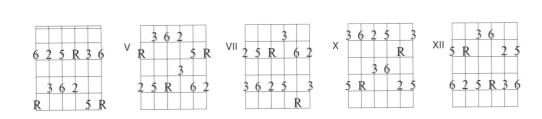

Figure B

A Pentatonic Minor Scale

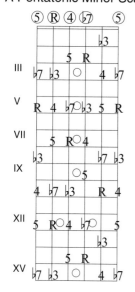
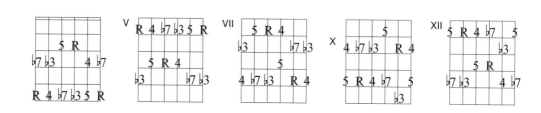

Figure C

A Blues Scale

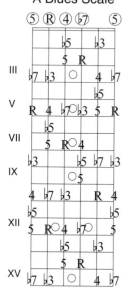
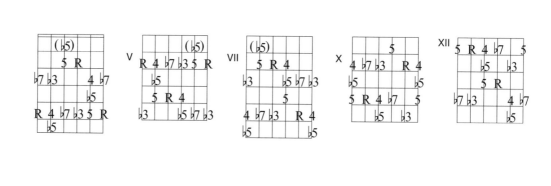

The 12-bar, I–IV–V-based progressions in Figures D and E provide the basic rhythmic and harmonic framework for most blues music. While the progressions are easily adaptable to 4/4 and 12/8 meters, the vast majority of examples in this volume are written in 12/8, which allows an accurate portrayal of eighth-note shuffle rhythms without the cumbersome triplet brackets, and accommodates a range of tempos from slow blues to medium up-tempo shuffles. If you haven't already done so, memorize both progressions. Figure D is a "slow-change" blues in *A*: four bars of the I (*A7*) chord, two bars of the IV (*D7*) chord, back to the I for two bars, the V (*E7*) chord for one bar, the IV (*D7*) chord for one bar, followed by two more bars of the I chord. Figure E is a "quick-change" blues in *A*, which adds more harmonic activity, namely a change to the IV chord in bar 2 and a busier I–IV–I–V (*A7–D7–A7–E7*) "turnaround" in bars 11 and 12. Unless otherwise indicated, the quick-change version shall be our standard progression of choice referenced throughout this book.

Figure D

Slow-change Blues

| $\frac{4}{4}$ or $\frac{12}{8}$ ‖: | A7 (I) | A7 (I) | A7 (I) | A7 (I) | D7 (IV) | D7 (IV) | A7 (I) | A7 (I) | E7 (V) | E7 (V) | A7 (I) | A7 (I) :‖ |

Figure E

Quick-change Blues

| $\frac{4}{4}$ or $\frac{12}{8}$ ‖: | A7 (I) | D7 (IV) | A7 (I) | A7 (I) | D7 (IV) | D7 (IV) | A7 (I) | A7 (I) | E7 (V) | D7 (IV) | A7 (I) D7 (IV) | A7 (I) E7 (V) :‖ |

If you play these three scales against each chord in either progression, you'll notice that some work with more than one chord and some do not. As a general rule, you'll find that the *A* pentatonic major scale works best with *A7* and *E7*, while the *A* pentatonic minor and *A* blues scales, which differ by only one additional note in the blues scale, get along equally well with every chord in either 12-bar progression. Of course, there are unlimited ways to mix elements from all three of these scales within a single lick, and that's one of the main talking points here at the Blues Lick Factory.

CHAPTER 2

TARGET TONES FAQ

What is a target tone? Here at the Blues Lick Factory, a target tone is, as the name implies, a predetermined or improvised single-note point of arrival that coincides harmonically with a specified chord within a 12-bar blues progression. In other words, it's a chord tone (root/1, 3, 5, ♭7) or suitable extension (♭3/#9 and 4/11 are our two choices, but 2/9 and 6/13 are also applicable) that belongs to or embellishes the I, IV, or V chords (*A7*, *D7*, and *E7* in the key of *A*) and falls on a strong, predetermined beat, usually the downbeat, or beat *one* of a measure. This translates to the following tones for each chord:

A7 (I) = *A* (root/1), *C#* (3), *E* (5), *G* (♭7), plus *C* (♭3/#9)

D7 (IV) = *D* (root/1), *F#* (3), *A* (5), *C* (♭7), plus *G* (4/11)

E7 (V) = *E* (root/1), *G#* (3), *B* (5), *D* (♭7), plus *G* (♭3/#9)

Why is it so important to hit the target? Because target tones lock you into the chord-of-the-moment and create the illusion of chordal accompaniment in your solos. When you hit a key chord tone on the downbeat of a chord change, you can actually define that chord with a single note regardless of what notes came before it (a key concept in jazz). However, some chord tones produce finer definition than others.

So which are the juiciest chord tones for target practice? The 3 and ♭7, which form a tritone interval (more on those in a minute), virtually define the dominant seventh quality of each chord, but tend to work best with the I and IV chords. (The 3 of the V chord [*G#* for *E7*] must be used judiciously in order to maintain a bluesy vibe, for instance by transposing a 3-heavy I-chord lick up three and one-half steps.) The root also works well with any chord, leaving the 5 as the least effective target tone. Our chosen extensions also provide very strong targets, with the ♭3/#9 carrying a bit more weight than the

4/11. But while this order of strongest-to-weakest chord tones applies to most music, the order of blues target tones tends to differ with the IV and V chords. While any tones will "work" on a technical level, some targets simply sound better than others. Here's our list of picks for the most- to least-bitchin' blues target tones in the key of A:

A7: 3, ♭7, 1, 5 (♭3/#9 is a very strong extension)

D7: ♭7, 3, 1, 5 (4/11 is a strong extension)

E7: 1, ♭7, 3, 5 (♭3/#9 is a very strong extension)

What are common tones? A7, D7, and E7 share many of the same chord tones and extensions and, as you'll soon discover, this is a beautiful thing. It should be noted that there are two ways to refer to any given note: by its relation to a key center, or by its relation to the chord-of-the-moment. Thus, A is the root/1 in the key of A and the root/1 of A7, but it is also the 5 of D7. Here's the scoop on common tones as they relate to each chord:

A = 1 of A7 (I); 5 of D7 (IV); 4/11 of E7 (V)

C = ♭3/#9 of A7 (I); ♭7 of D7 (IV); #5/♭6 of E7 (V)

C# = 3 of A7 (I); 6/13 of E7 (V)

D = 1 of D7 (IV); ♭7 of E7 (V); 4/11 of A7 (I)

E = 5 of A7 (I); 1 of E7 (V); E = 2/9 of D7 (IV)

F# = 3 of D7 (IV); 6 of A7 (I); 2/9 of E7 (V)

G = ♭7 of A7 (I); 4/11 of D7 (IV); ♭3/#9 of E7 (V)

G# = 3 of E7 (V)

B = 5 of E7 (V); B = 2/9 of A7 (I); 6/13 of D7 (IV)

As you can see, there are only a few target tones that don't work for all three chords. The important ones to avoid are C# over D7—that's the major 7 against a dominant seventh chord—and G# over A7 for the same reason, though you'll soon discover that both may be used as passing tones if they are played on weak beats.

And what about that bluest of blue notes, the ♭5? Truth be told, the ♭5 (*Eb* in the key of *A*) is a full-fledged member of the *A* blues scale and an excellent passing tone that works well with all three chords. But, unless you happen to be shooting for say, *F7*, the ♭VI chord in the key of *A*—which may be substituted for the V chord in bar 9 of many minor blues progressions—the ♭5 makes a lousy target and has been excluded from this list. (Tip: For 12-bar quick-change or slow-change minor blues progressions, substitute minor or minor seventh chords for all three changes [*Am(7)*, *Dm(7)*, and *Em(7)*] or use a dominant seventh V chord [*E7*] throughout. If you sub a ♭VI7 for the V7 in bar 9 as described above, follow it with a V7 chord in bar 10.)

Where do I find these tones? Glad you asked! Figure F compiles three octaves of every chord tone present in the I, IV, and V chords in the key of *A*—our global tonal center used throughout this book— plus a tasty extension for each one into a parental *A* blues target-tone scale. The relationship of each note in this parent scale to each chord in a standard 12-bar blues in *A* is defined by three sets of numbers written between the standard notation and TAB systems. Circled numbers are chord tones (1, 3, 5, and ♭7), parenthesized numbers indicate extensions (♭3/#9 for the I and V chords, and 4/11 for the IV chord), and the untouched numbers are tones that will not work over one or more of the chords. Get to know them and you'll eventually learn the sound of each tone and how it behaves with each chord so you can let go of all of this technical jargon and just react intuitively. (Advance Tip: You'll find every note in every tritone and seventh-chord voicing from Figures G through M present in this list of target tones.)

Figure F

Blues Target Tones (Key of A)

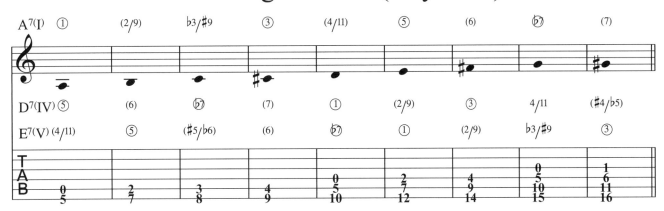

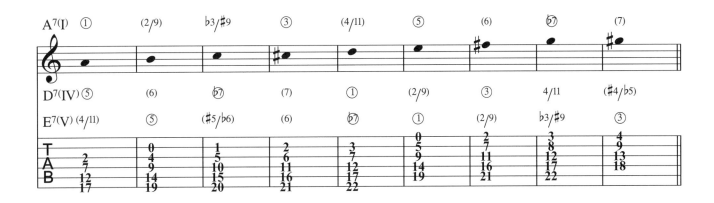

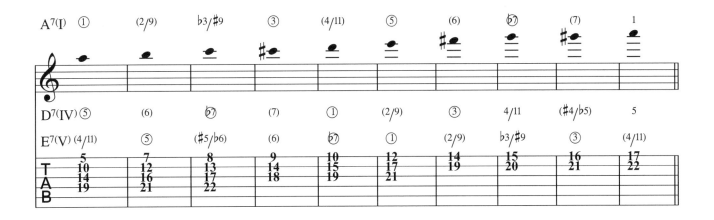

A great way to memorize multiple locations of notes on the fretboard is to make your own full fingerboard grids of all occurrences of any given note. For instance, if you place all of the A's up to and including the twelfth fret on a grid (6th-string/5th-fret, 5th-string/open and 12th-fret, 4th-string/7th-fret, 3rd-string/2nd-fret, 2nd-string/ 10th-fret, and 1st-string/5th-fret) you'll discover that they combine to form an overall fretboard pattern, or note matrix. This matrix, which repeats itself above the twelfth fret, can be moved along the entire neck to locate all existing fretted positions of any given note, and the notes in the matrix always retain the same fretboard shape in relation to each other. Think of the matrix as a constellation of notes—especially if you connect the dots—that maintains its shape regardless of its position in space. Once committed to memory, this overall fretboard pattern can be referenced from any note or set of notes within the 12-fret matrix. (For more on the note matrix and the duplication of tones on the fingerboard, see *The Guitar Cookbook*.)

How and when do I use target tones? You can apply I (*A7*) chord targets on the downbeat, or beat *one* of bars 1, 3, 4, 7, 8, and 11 (add 2 and 12 during slow-change progressions), IV (*D7*) chord targets on the downbeat of bars 2, 5, 6, and 11(omit 2 during slow-change progressions), and V(*E7*) chord targets on the bars 9 and 12 (omit 12 during slow-change progressions). Play them in any octave and decorate them with as many phrasing ornaments (bends, hammer-ons, pull-offs, slides, etc.) as you like.

How should I practice target tones? Before you start applying them to licks, familiarize yourself with your options for each chord by playing through a 12-bar *A* blues progression using nothing *but* target tones played as dotted whole notes on beat *one* of each measure, that is, sustained for an entire bar of 12/8. Start with all roots (*A, D,* and *E*), then try all 3's (*C#, F#,* and *G#*), all 5's (*E, A,* and *B*), and all ♭7's (*G, C,* and *D*) before mixing them up in various configurations: try the 3 (*C#*) for *A7*, and the ♭7's (*C* and *D*) for *D7* and *E7*, or reverse this strategy to the ♭7 (*G*) for *A7* and the 3's (*F#* and *G#*) for *D7* and *E7*. Additionally, you can experiment with more than one target tone during adjacent bars of the same chord.

Who cares? Your audience. Target tones allow you to lead the listener though a chord progression using only a series of single notes, a trait usually associated with jazz but equally applicable to blues. Your fans will love you for it.

CHAPTER 3

TRITONES AND SEVENTH-CHORD VOICINGS

A musical interval, or the distance between two notes, is measured in half-step (one fret on the guitar) and whole-step increments (two frets). The tritone, or flatted fifth (two notes played three whole steps apart), may be the most important interval in blues music. When these two notes are sounded simultaneously, they produce the essential tones in a dominant seventh chord, the *3* and the *♭7*. These two key chord tones are all you need to form the I7, IV7, and V7 chords in any standard 12-bar blues progression. Like any musical interval, the tritone forms a distinctive shape on the fingerboard, in this case a diagonal "slash" shape across two strings that is easily transferable to any other set of adjacent strings. Figures G, H, and I illustrate two octaves of tritone intervals derived from the I7 (*A7*), IV7 (*D7*), and V7 (*E7*) chords in the key of *A*, the global key center utilized throughout this book. Each one functions as a partial dominant seventh chord. Get to know them.

Figure G

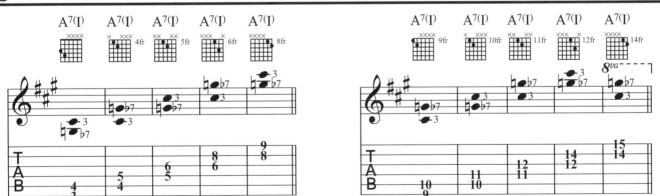

Figure H

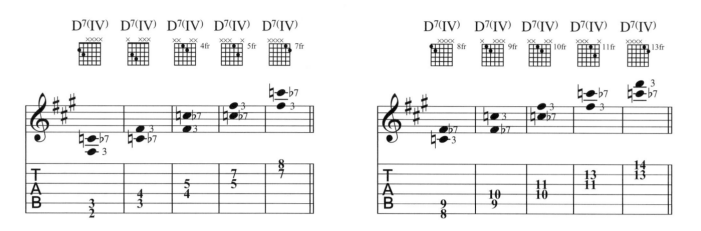

Figure I

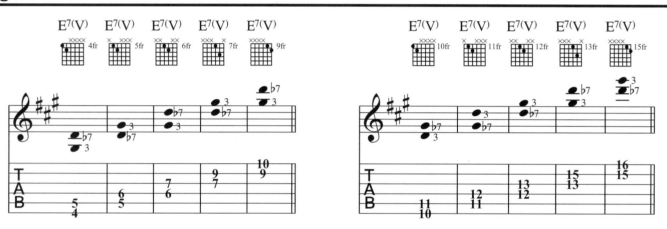

Notice how the tones reverse—from ♭7 over 3 to 3 over ♭7—as each tritone is inverted to include the next higher string. This is a beautiful thing that makes it possible to form partial IV7 and V7 chords simply by lowering or raising any I-chord tritone one half-step. Figure J shows how to locate the *D7* and *E7* tritones one half-step below and above the previous *A7* tritones. For variety, try moving any A7 tritone up a perfect fourth interval (two and one-half steps) to form D7, either on the same strings or by crossing to the next string group at the same fret position and an additional whole step, or perfect fifth, higher for *E7*. Another way to accomplish the latter is to use the I-chord tritone from any example and the IV- and V-chord tritones from an adjacent example. (Tip: This also works with the upcoming three- and four-note seventh-chord voicings.) And don't forget to raise all notes on the *B* string one half-step to compensate for the guitar's pesky tuning system.

Figure J

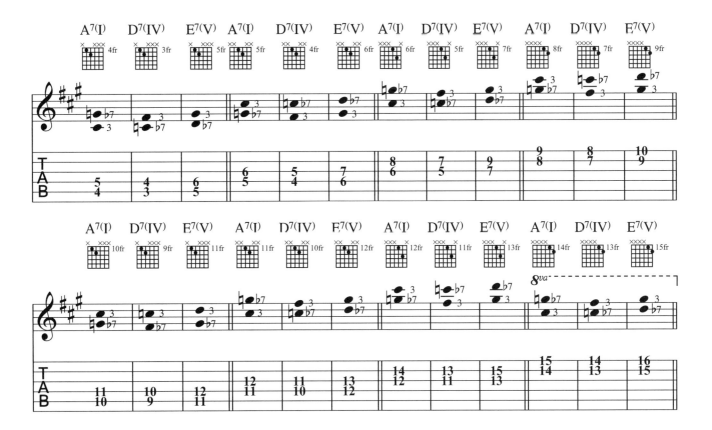

For a thicker sound, use the hip three- and four-note *A7*, *D7*, and *E7* voicings depicted in Figures K, L, and M. Keep in mind that you can also raise any *A7* voicing a perfect fourth or fifth to form *D7* and *E7*, just as we did with the tritones. (Hint: Adopting a general rule to steer clear of those borderline cornball five- and six-note barred seventh-chord voicings will keep your comping cool, crisp, and to the point.)

Figure K

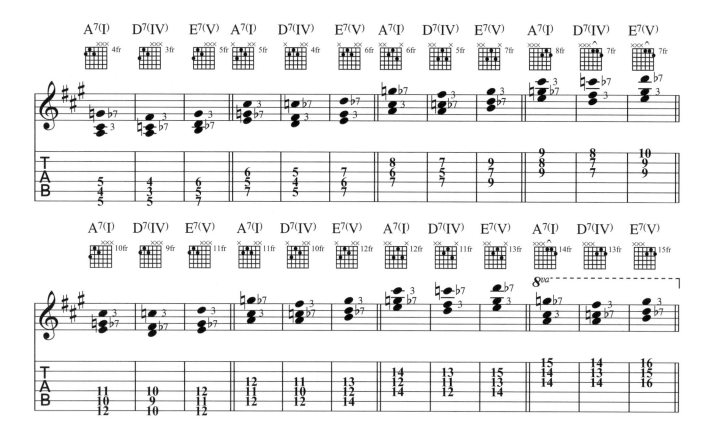

Figure L

Figure M

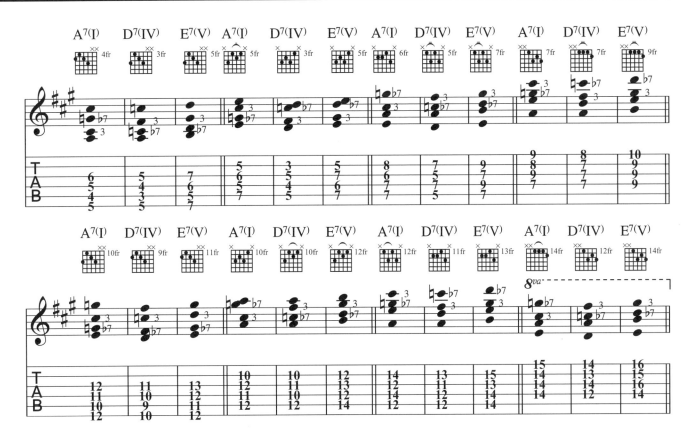

Between tritones and three- and four-note seventh-chord voicings, you now have the necessary tools to comp through nearly any standard 12-bar blues progression in the key of A. Once you know these smooth moves well enough, start transposing them to different keys.

CHAPTER 4

THREE-NOTE PICKUP LICKS

More than half of the new *Blues Lick Factory* is dedicated to the production of our world-famous line of D.I.Y. lick modules. We've had such good response to the flagship models produced in the original *Guitar Lick Factory* that we've decided to retool them with the addition of fifteen optional target tones. Now you'll have more than a dozen options for how to resolve each three-, four-, five-, or six-note lick so you can use them with any chord in a standard 12-bar *A* blues progression. And while all of our stock models utilize the same three-, four-, five-, and six-note rhythmic motifs to facilitate easier reading and retention, you can customize each one by visiting our "Rhythmic Variations" division for all of your metric needs. (See Examples 110a–j through 118a–h.)

Essentially, you'll be on your own without any narrative distractions for the next 109 licks (actually, with five optional targets per chord, it's more like 109×15), but fear not: each lick, plus all of its optional target tones, is demonstrated on the accompanying audio disc. For your convenience, all example numbers match their respective track numbers, and a tuning reference can be found on track 198. Now let's get this assembly line rolling!

Examples 1 through 32 should be broken in as pickup licks, i.e., placed on the last beat in a bar of 12/8. Begin each three-note lick on beat *four* to approach your choice of target tones on the downbeat, or beat *one* of the next measure. The idea is to use the I (*A7*) chord target tones to approach the downbeats of bars 1, 3, 4, 7, 8, or 11 (adding bars 2 and 12 during slow-change progressions), the IV (*D7*) chord target tones to approach the downbeats of bars 2, 5, 6, or 10 (omitting bar 2 and 12 during slow-change progressions), and the V (*E7*) chord target tones to approach the downbeats of bars 9 or 12 (omitting bar 12 during slow-change progressions). All of the preceding also goes for the upcoming five- and six-note pickup licks in 3/8, and can be adjusted to pertain to our four-note pickups in 2/4. (See Examples 110a–j and 111a–h for a slew of optional three-note rhythmic variations.)

On the disc: The "a," "b," and "c" segments of each 3/8 example have been combined on a single track. (Keep in mind that all of these three-note pickup modules were designed to begin on beat *four* when applied to a measure of 12/8.) Here's how it works: A three-beat countoff, with each dotted-quarter beat containing three eighth notes, precedes the "a" lick played into the I chord, which establishes its tonality. This is immediately followed by the same lick played into each I-chord target tone, then the same process is repeated—minus the three-beat countoff—in time and without interruption for the "b" and "c" examples using the IV- and V-chords (*D7* and *E7*) and their respective target tones, which means that there are essentially fifteen licks on each track. Confusing? Maybe a little, but after much research we decided that this was the best way to present this plethora of target tone options for every lick.

Track 1

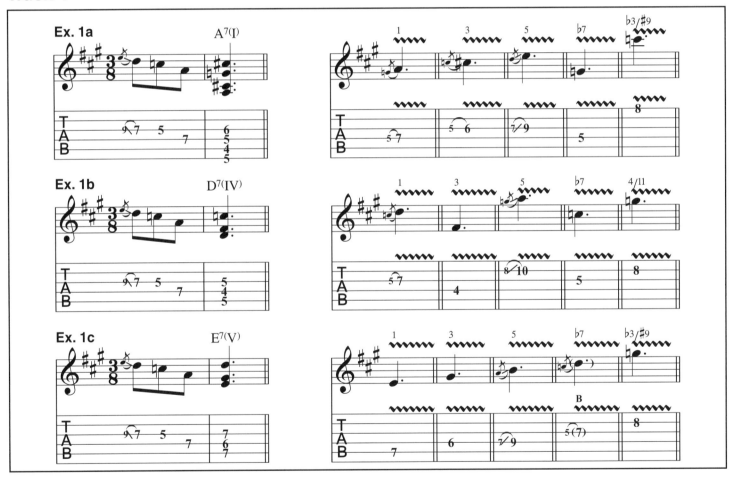

Track 2

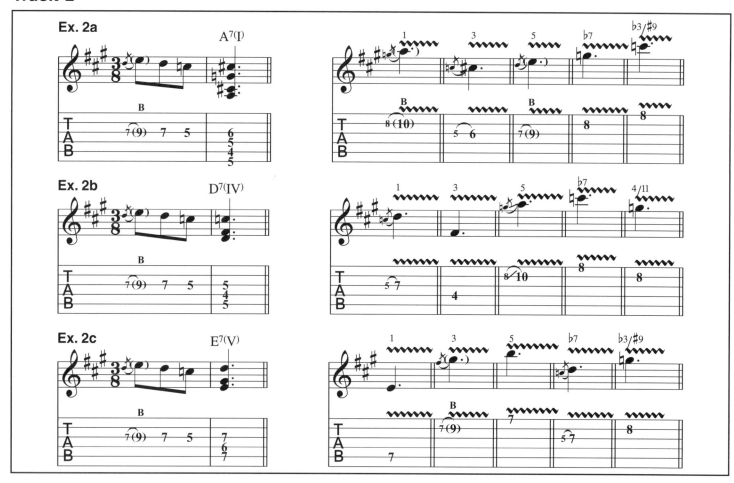

Track 3

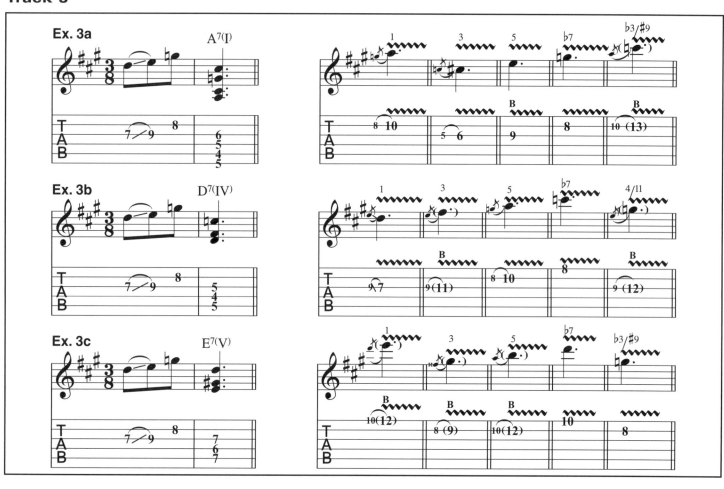

Track 4

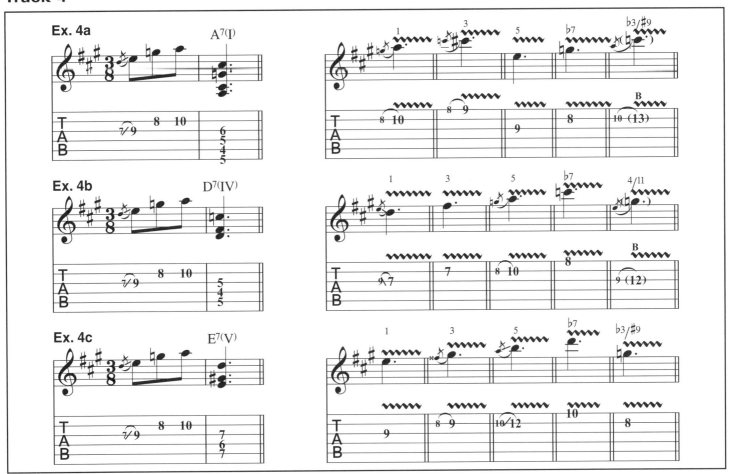

Track 5

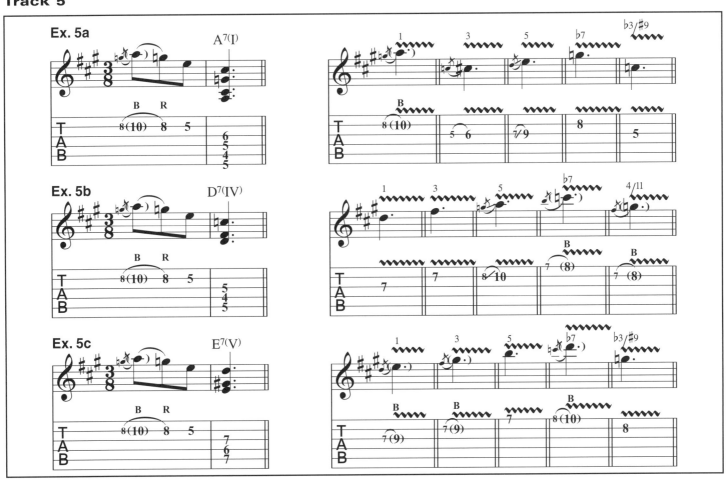

Track 6

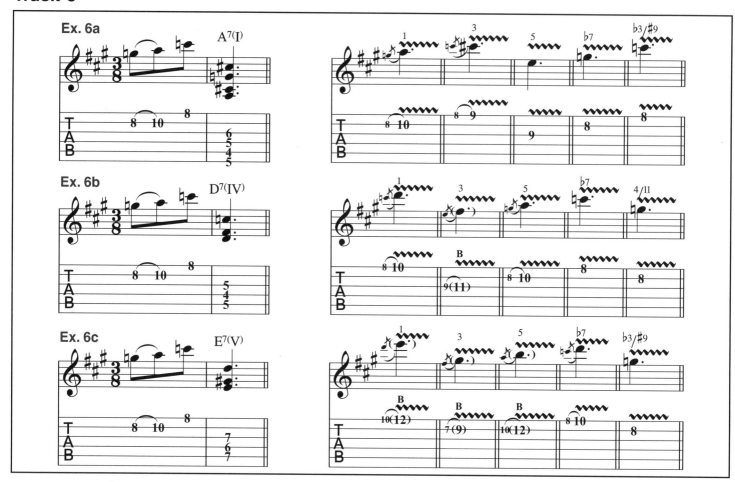

Track 7

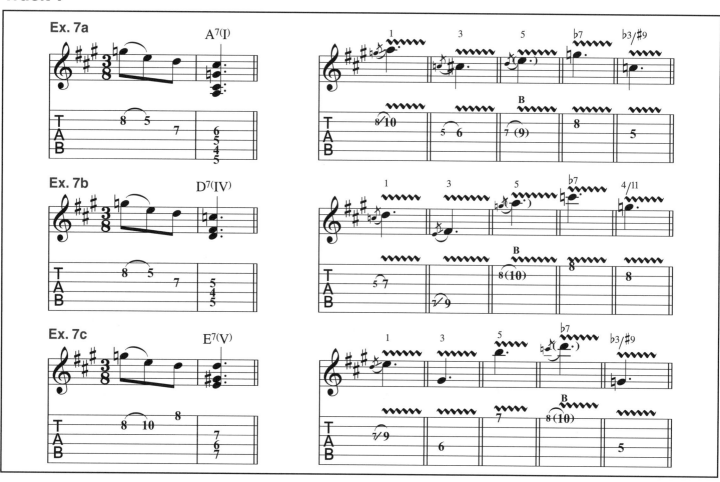

Track 8

Track 9

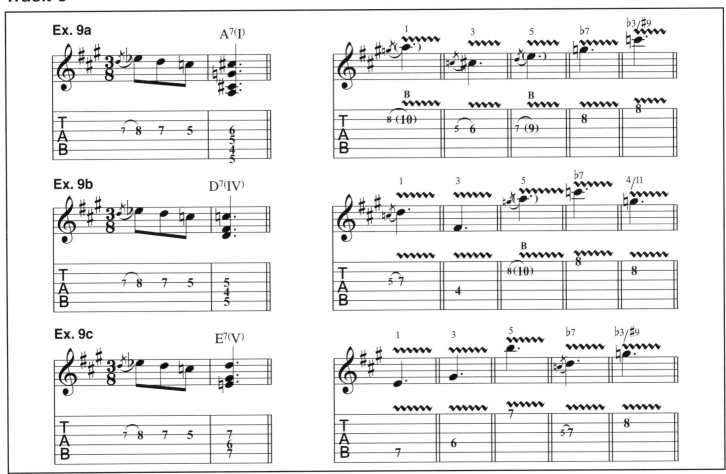

Track 10

Ex. 10a

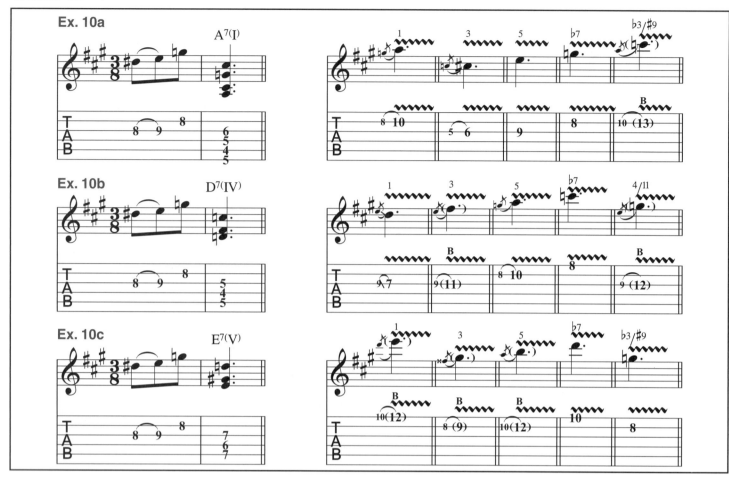

Ex. 10b

Ex. 10c

Track 11

Ex. 11a

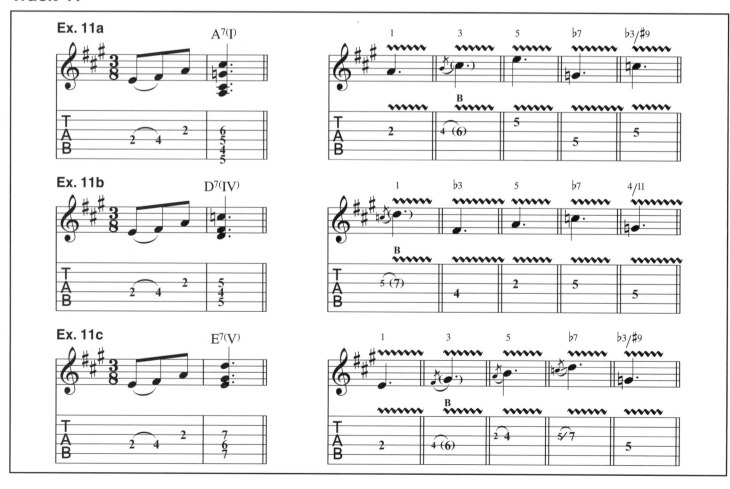

Ex. 11b

Ex. 11c

Track 12

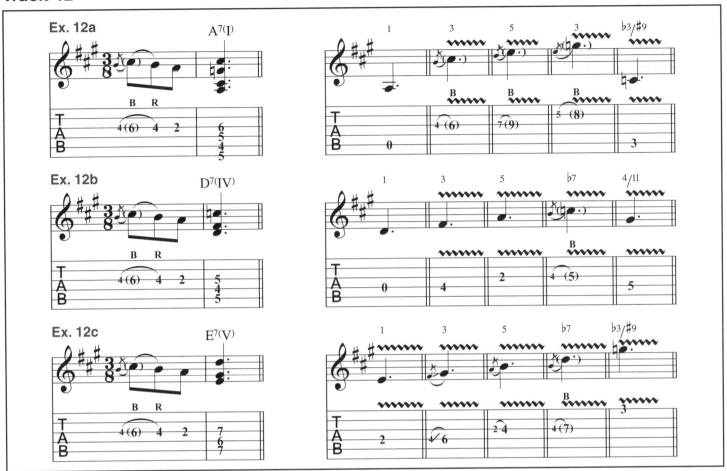

Track 13

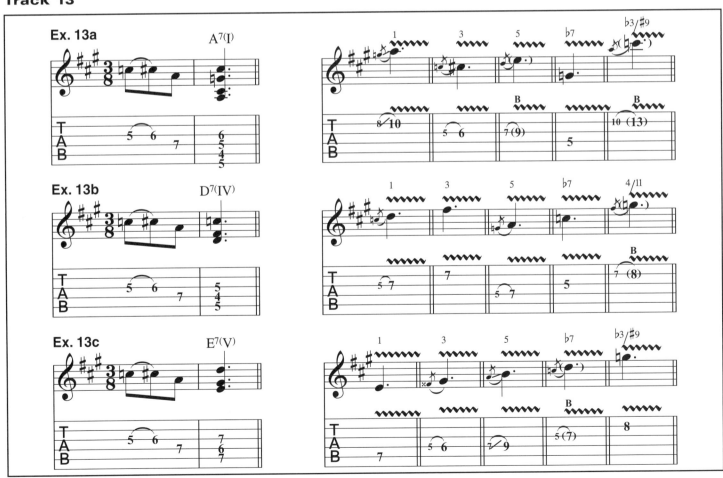

Track 14

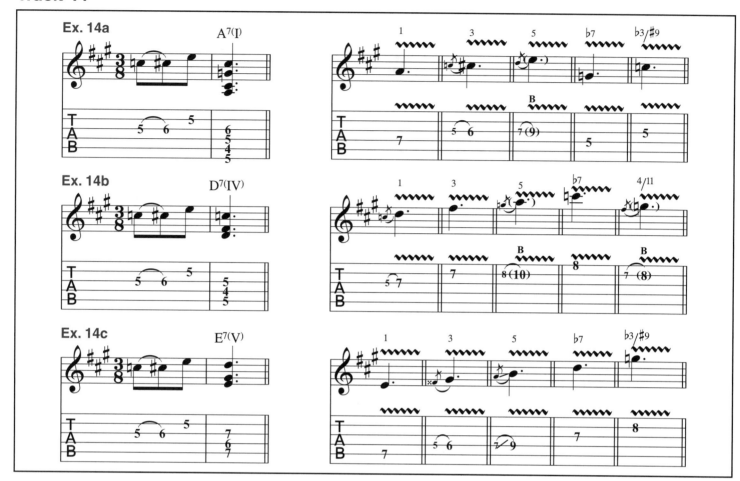

Track 15

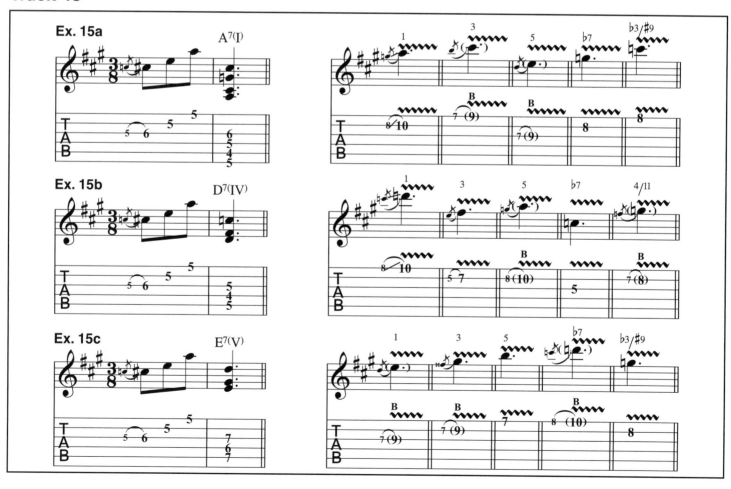

Track 16

Track 17

Track 18

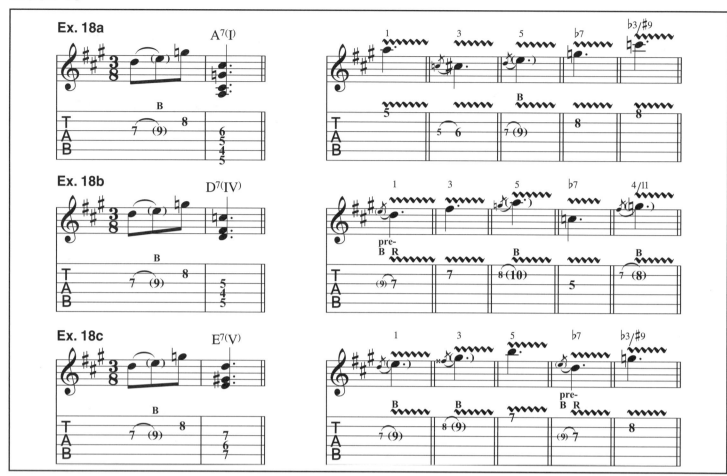

Track 19

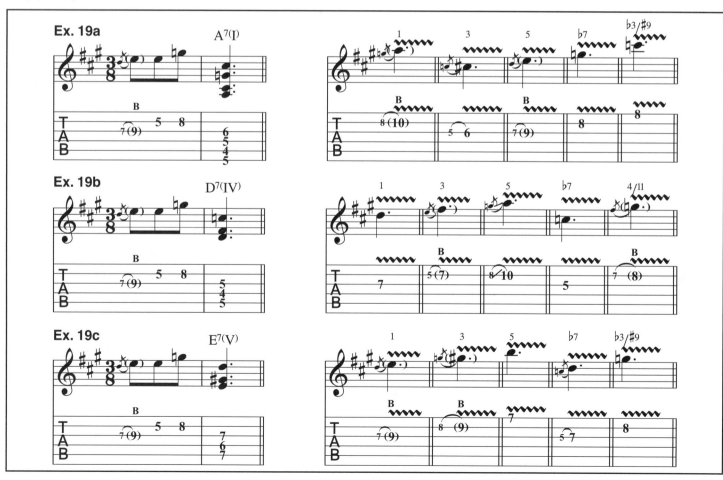

Track 20

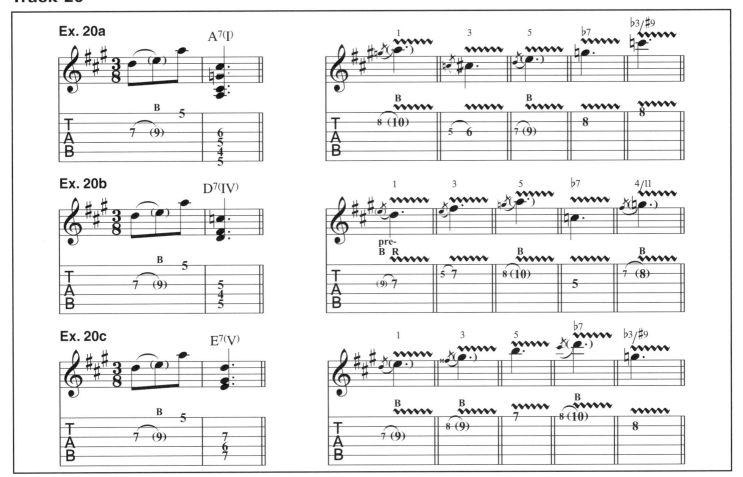

Track 21

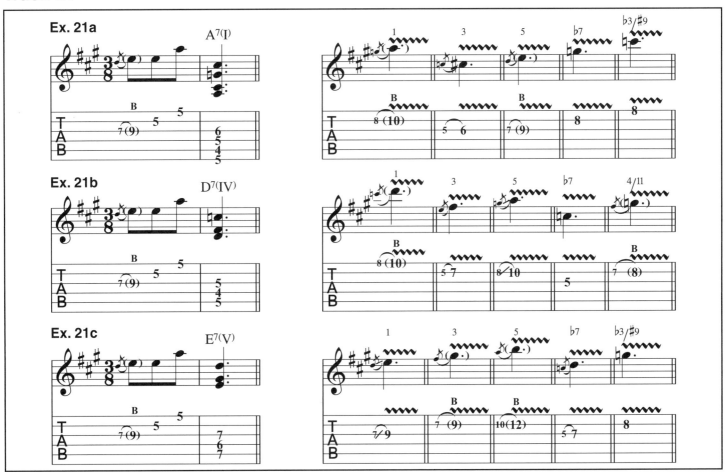

Track 22

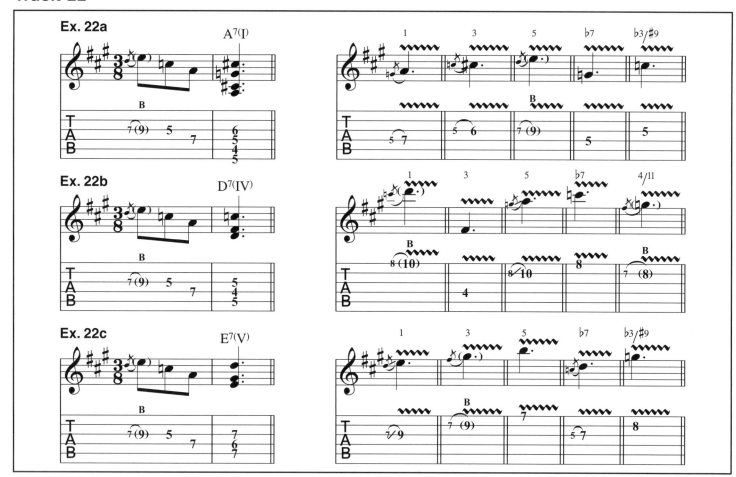

Track 23

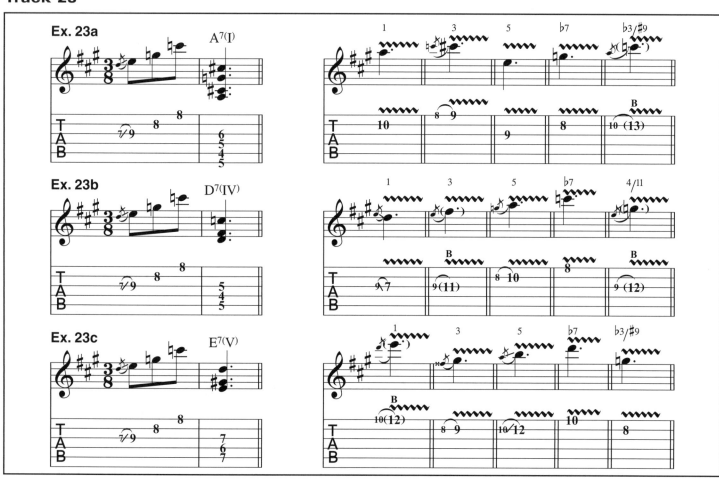

Track 24

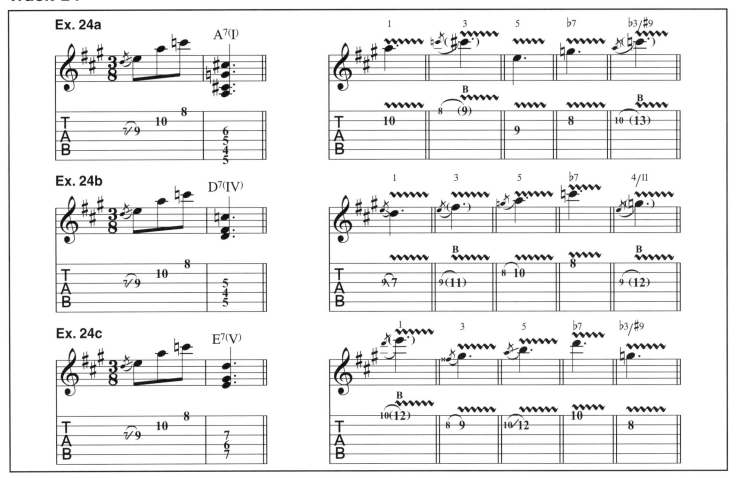

Track 25

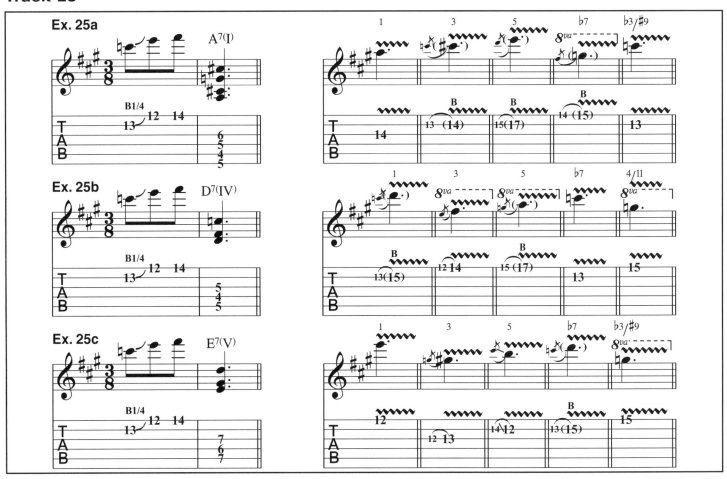

Track 26

Track 27

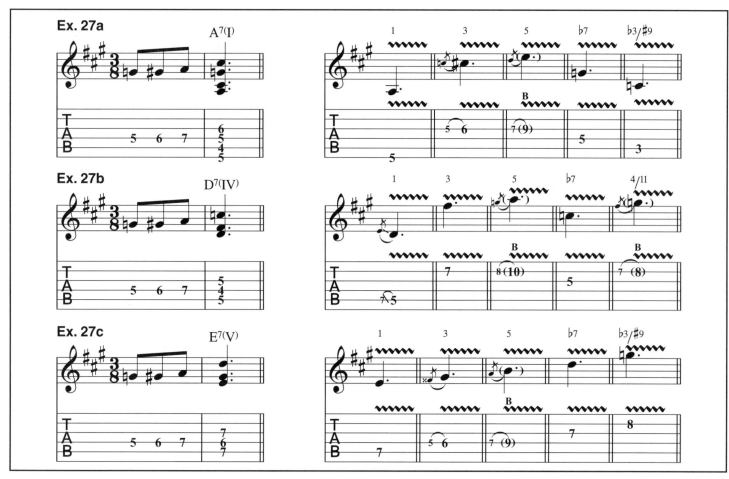

Track 28

Ex. 28a

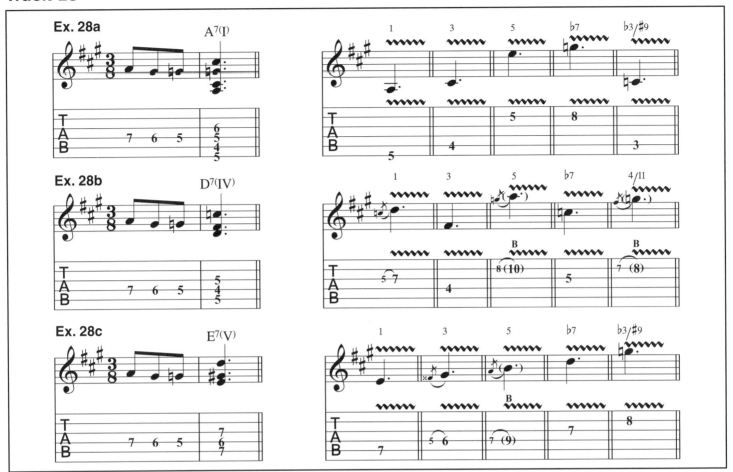

Track 29

Ex. 29a

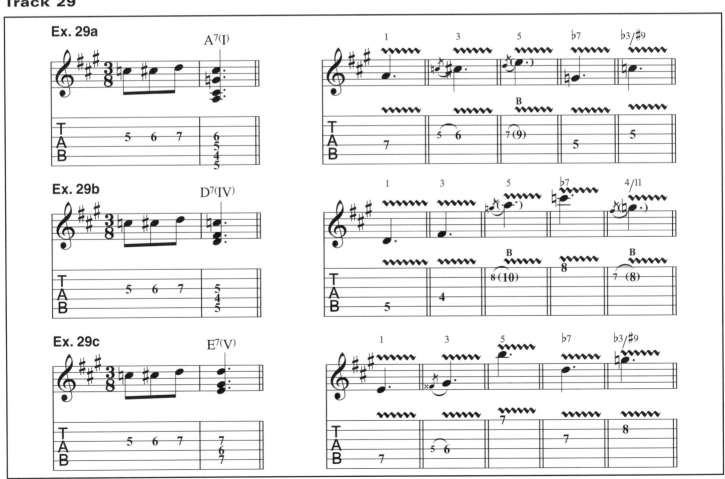

Track 30

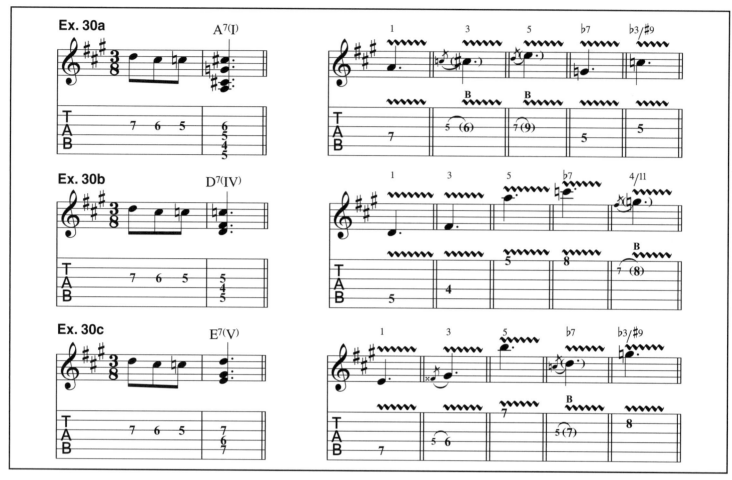

Ex. 30a

Ex. 30b

Ex. 30c

Track 31

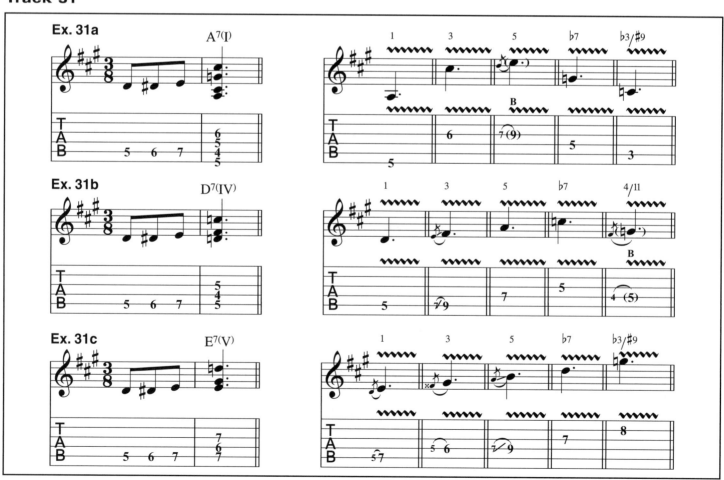

Ex. 31a

Ex. 31b

Ex. 31c

Track 32

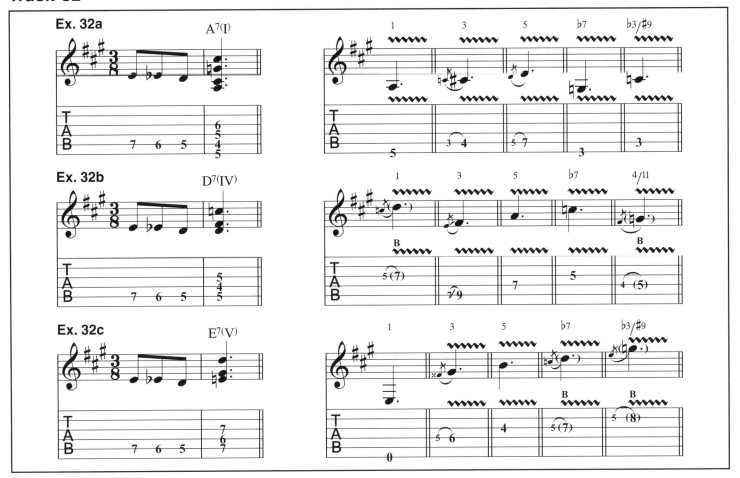

CHAPTER 5

FOUR-NOTE PICKUP LICKS

All of our four-note pickups are notated as consecutive eighth notes in 2/4, but if you would prefer them in 3/8, simply convert them into two sixteenth notes followed by two eighths. Be sure to visit our "Rhythmic Variations" department for more 3/8 and 2/4 options. (See Examples 112a–k and 113a–j.)

On the disc: The "a," "b," and "c" segments of each 2/4 example have been combined on a single track, and the tempo has been adjusted to accommodate the 2/4 meter. (Keep in mind that all of these four-note pickup modules were designed to begin on beat *three* when applied to a measure of 4/4.) Here's how it works: A six-beat countoff, with each quarter-note beat containing two eighth notes, precedes the "a" lick played into the I chord, which establishes its tonality. This is immediately followed by the same lick played into each I-chord target tone. Then the same process is repeated—minus the six-beat countoff—in time and without interruption for the "b" and "c" examples using the IV- and V-chords (*D7* and *E7*) and their respective target tones.

Track 33

Ex. 33a

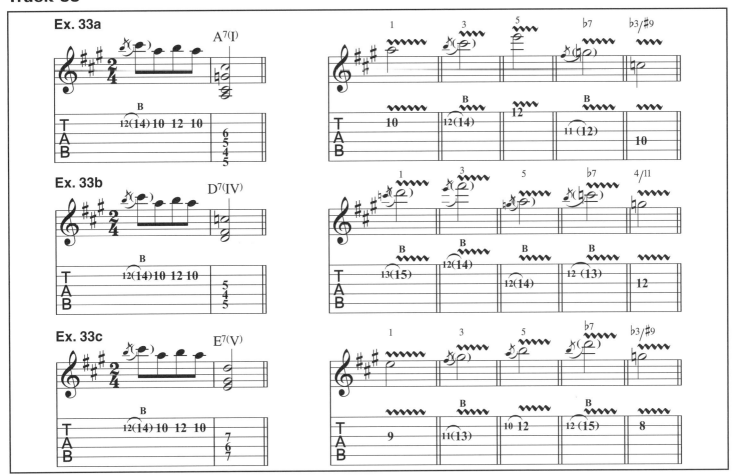

Track 34

Ex. 34a

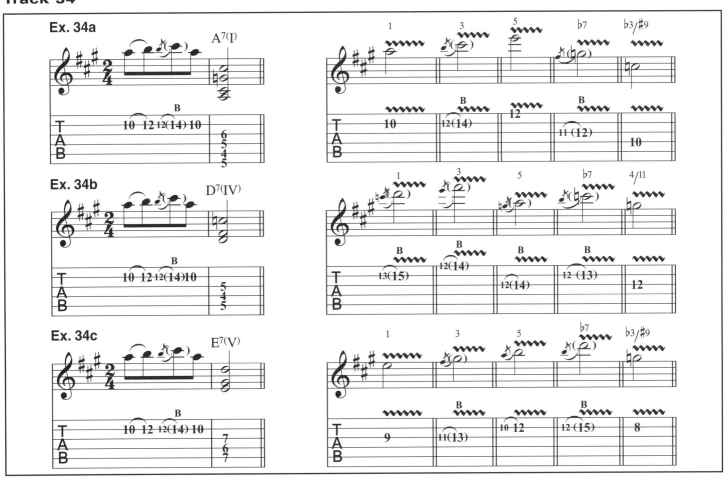

Track 35

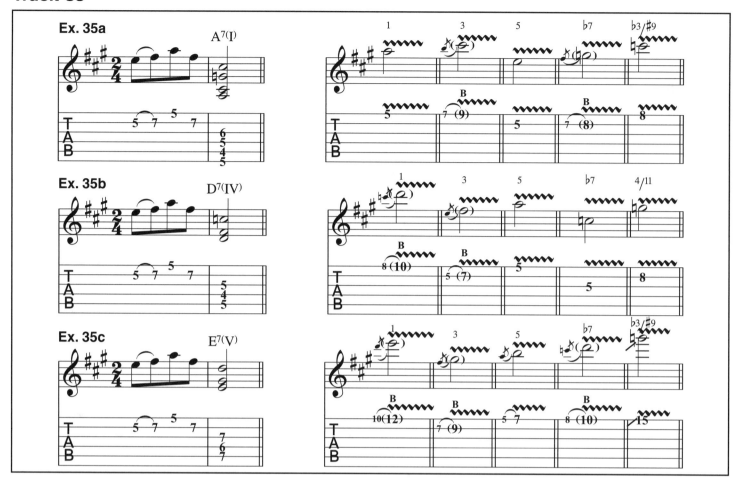

Track 36

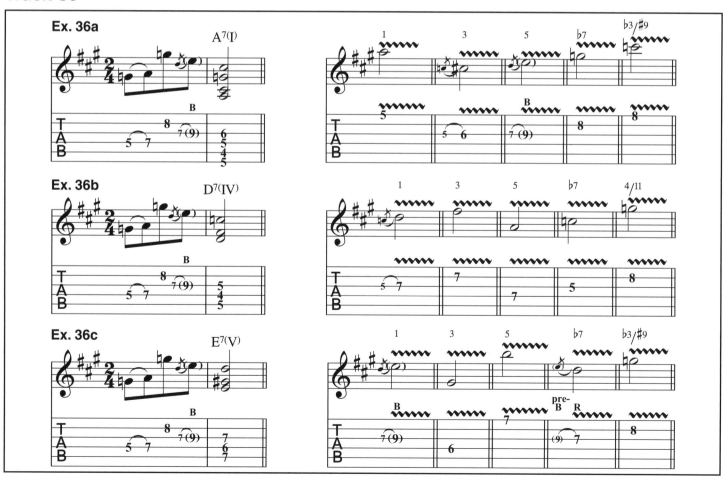

Track 37

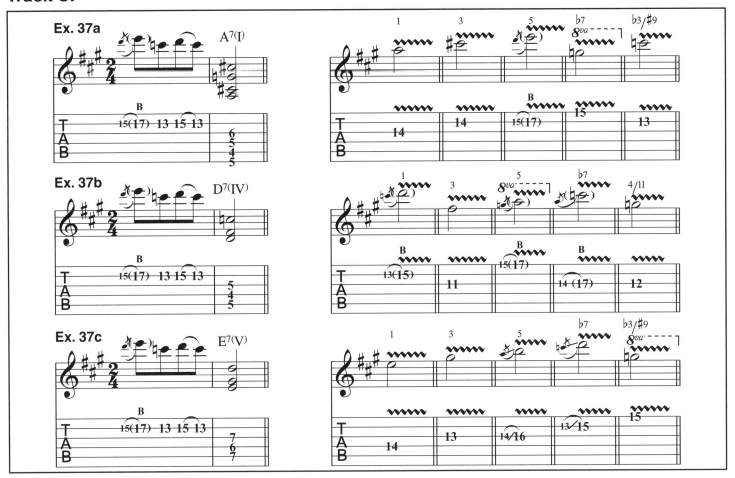

Track 38

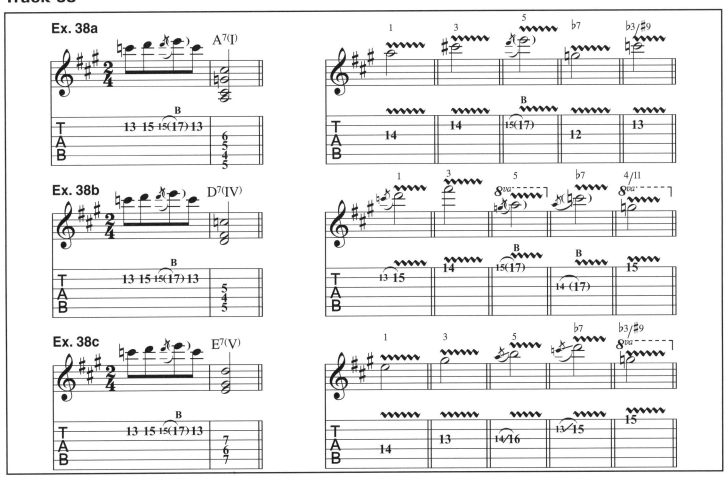

Track 39

Ex. 39a

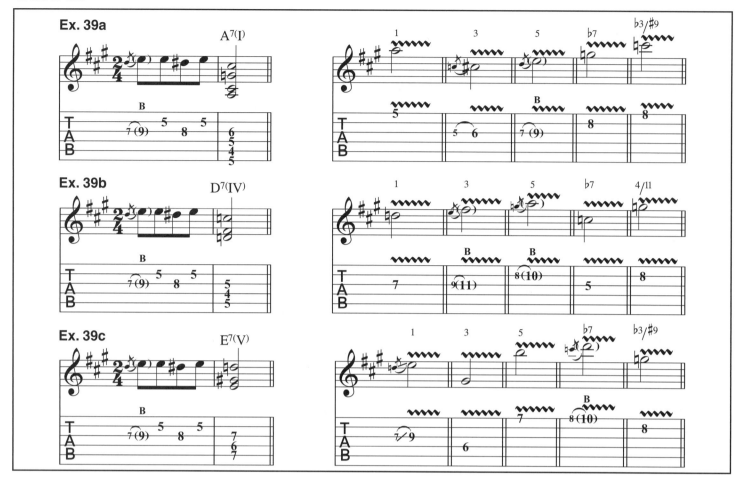

Ex. 39b

Ex. 39c

Track 40

Ex. 40a

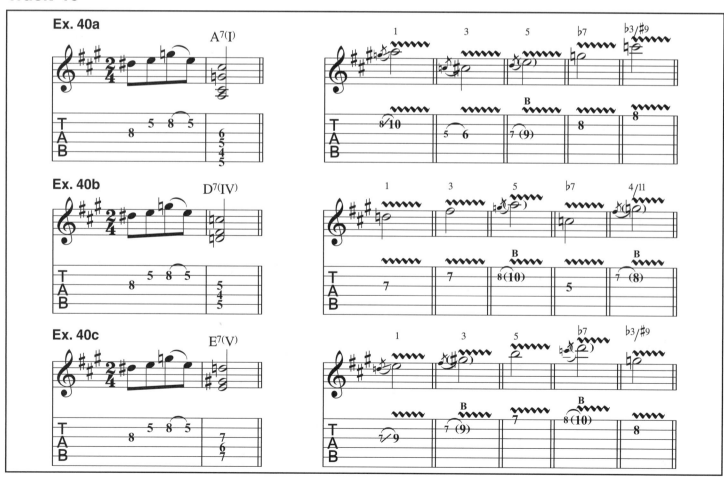

Ex. 40b

Ex. 40c

Track 41

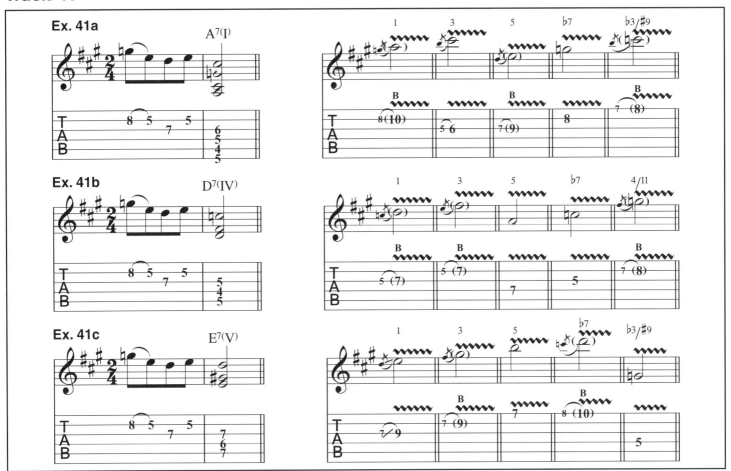

Track 42

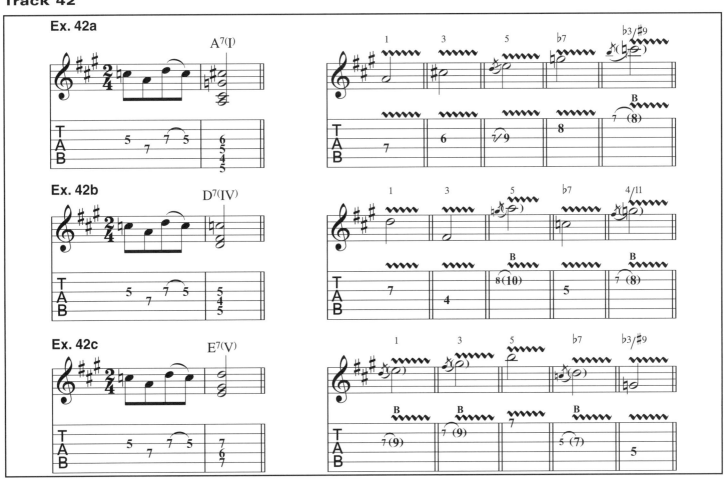

Track 43

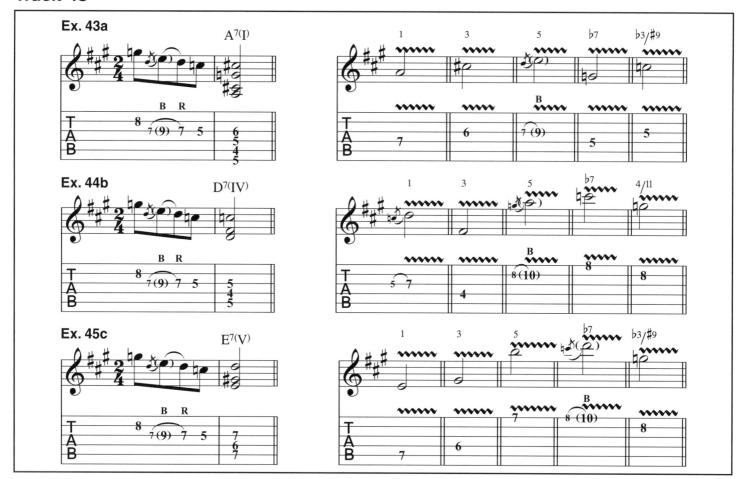

Ex. 43a

A⁷(I)

Ex. 44b

D⁷(IV)

Ex. 45c

E⁷(V)

Track 44

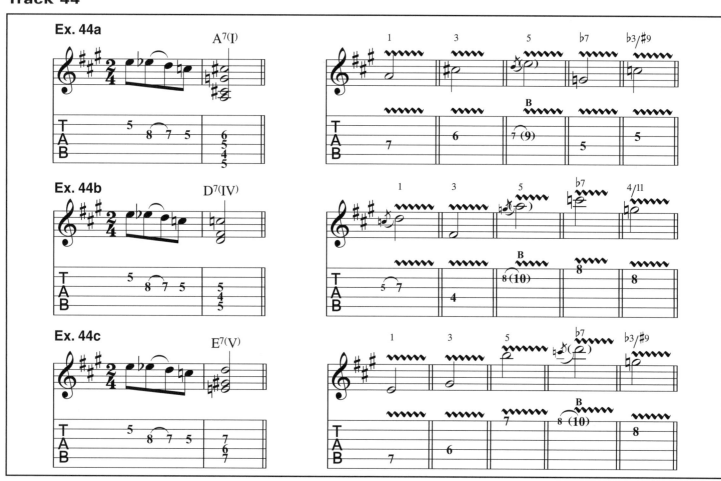

Ex. 44a

A⁷(I)

Ex. 44b

D⁷(IV)

Ex. 44c

E⁷(V)

Track 45

Ex. 45a

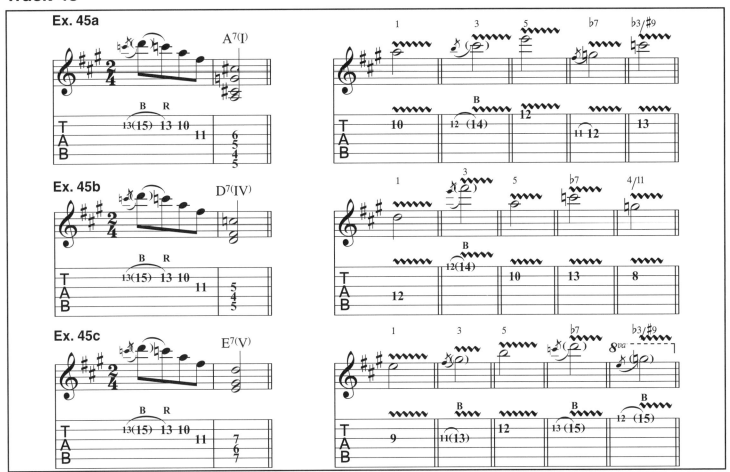

Track 46

Ex. 46a

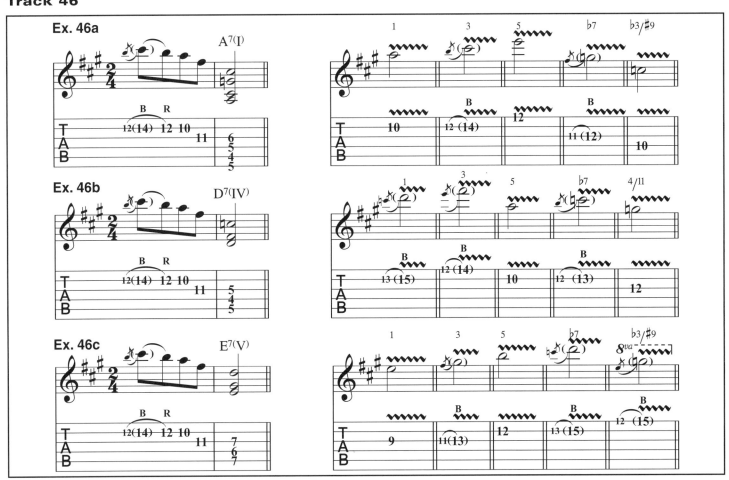

Track 47

Ex. 47a

Ex. 47b

Ex. 47c

Track 48

Ex. 48a

Ex. 48b

Ex. 48c

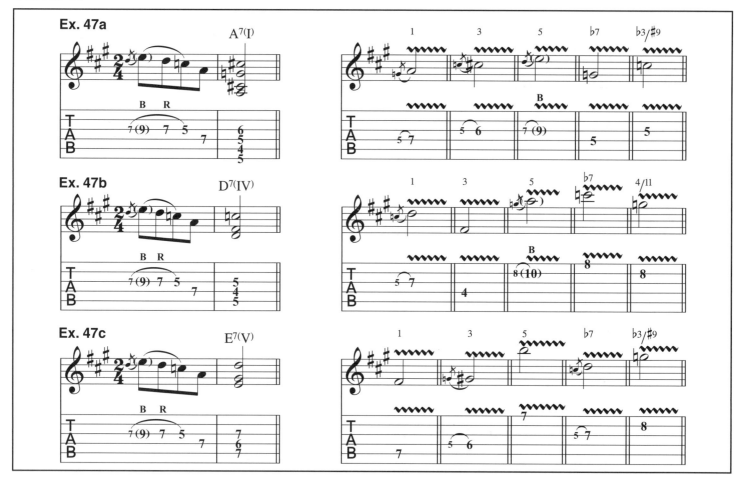

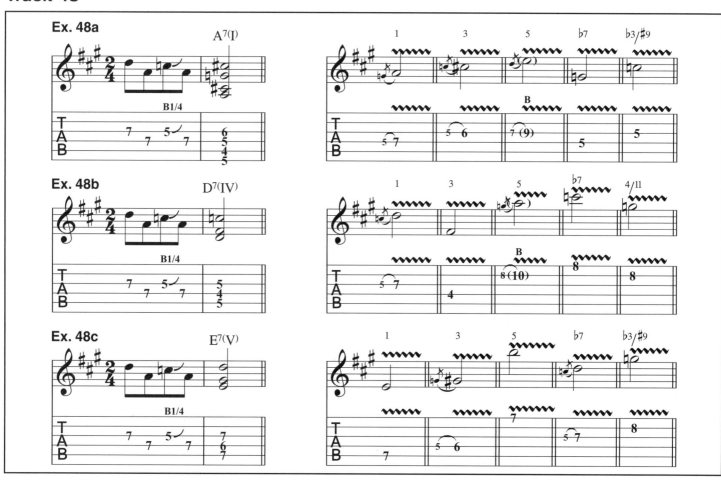

Track 49

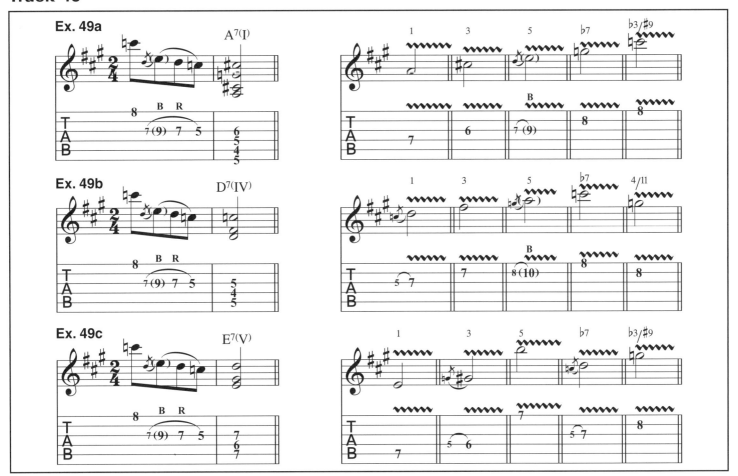

Ex. 49a

Ex. 49b

Ex. 49c

Track 50

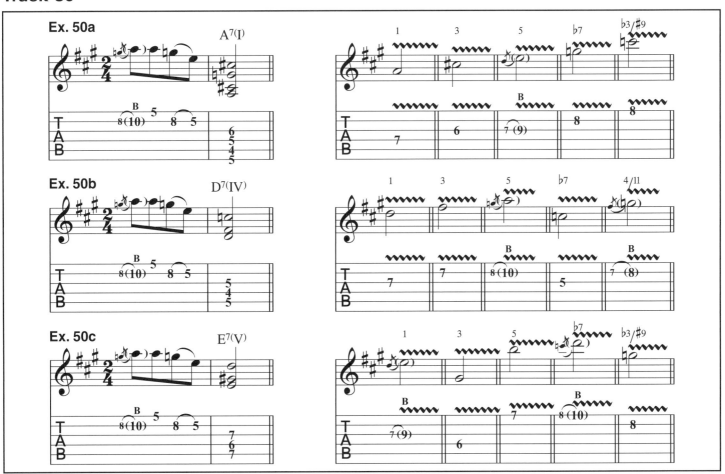

Ex. 50a

Ex. 50b

Ex. 50c

Track 51

Ex. 51a

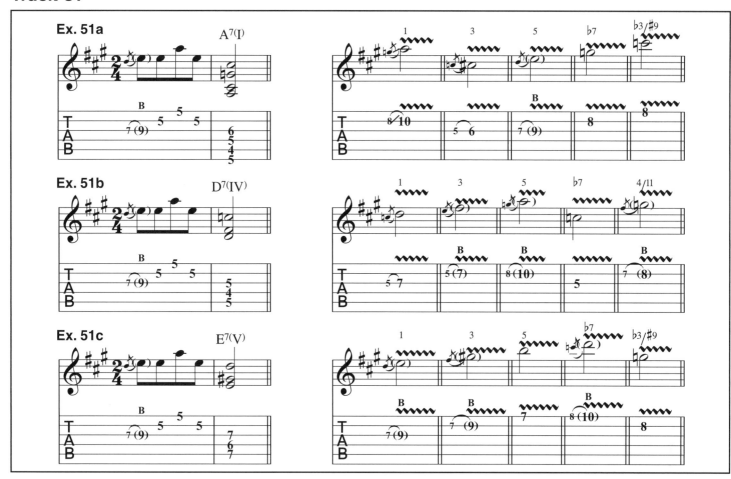

Ex. 51b

Ex. 51c

Track 52

Ex. 52a

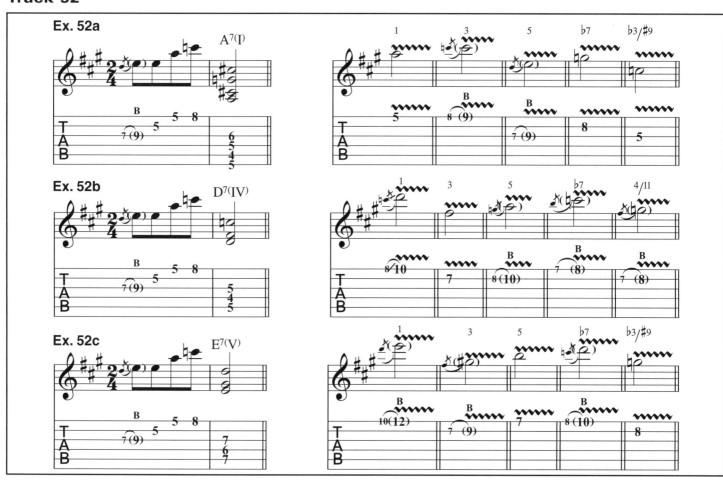

Ex. 52b

Ex. 52c

Track 53

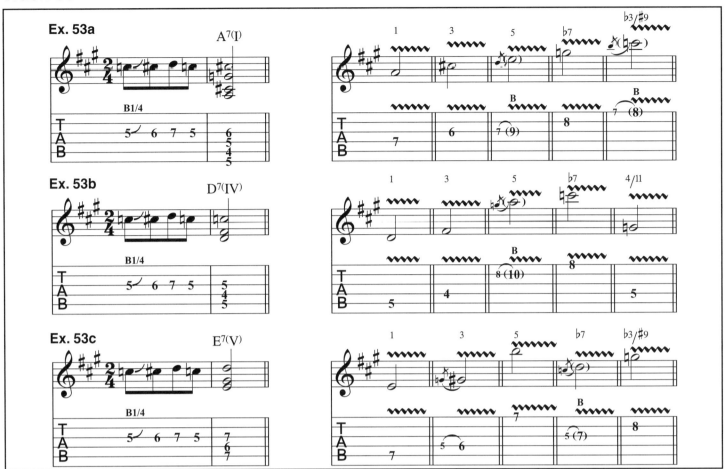

Track 54

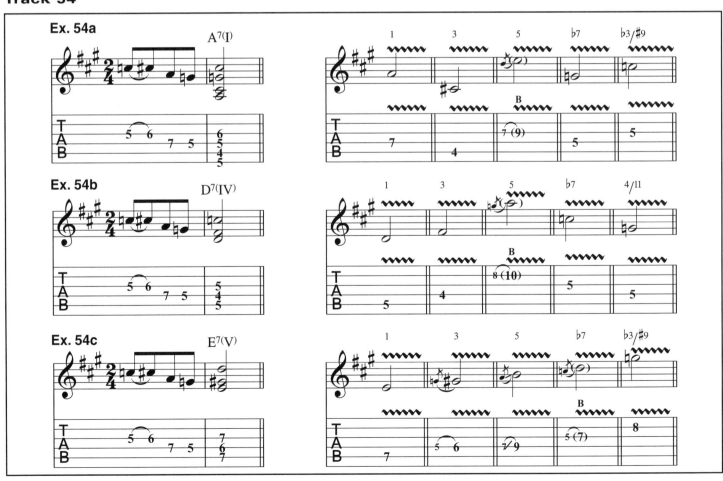

Track 55

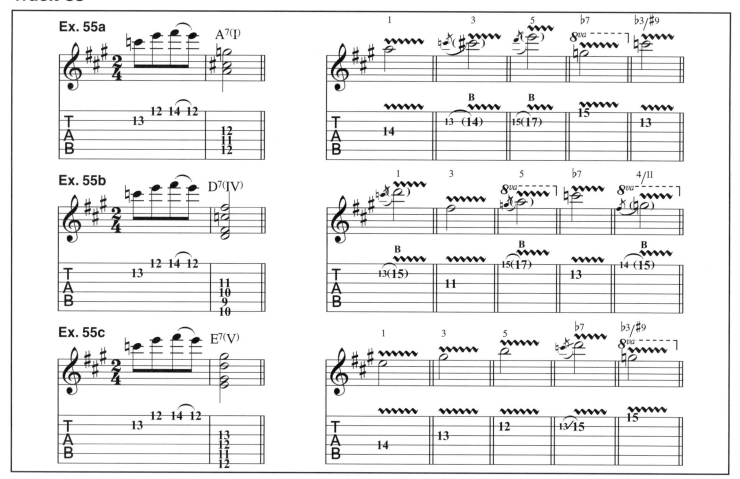

Track 56

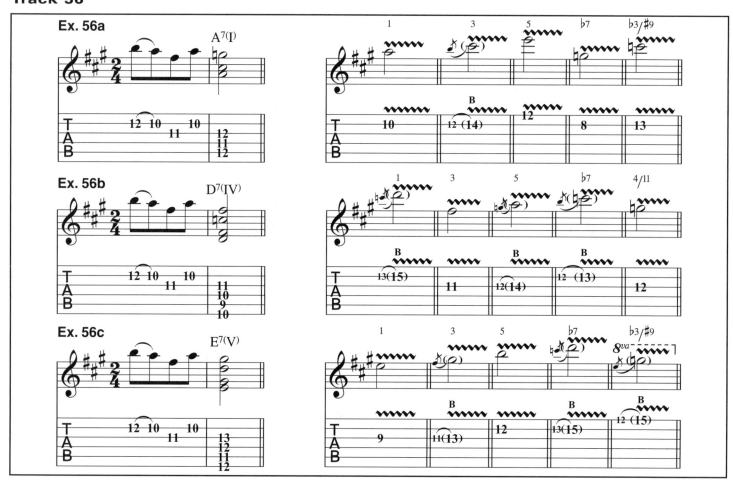

Track 57

Ex. 57a

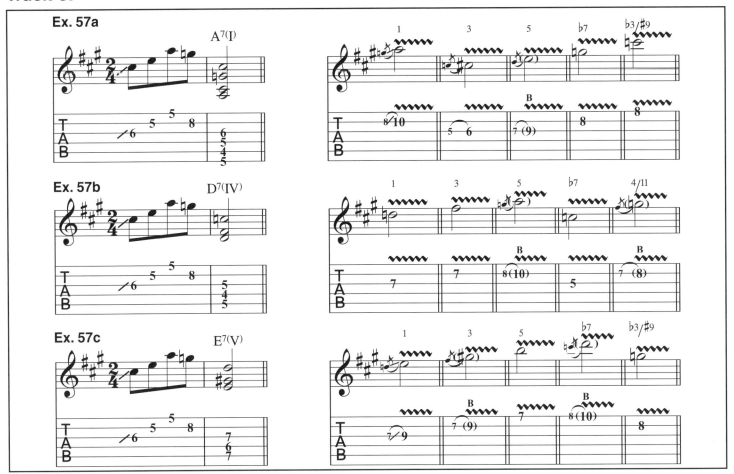

Ex. 57b

Ex. 57c

Track 58

Ex. 58a

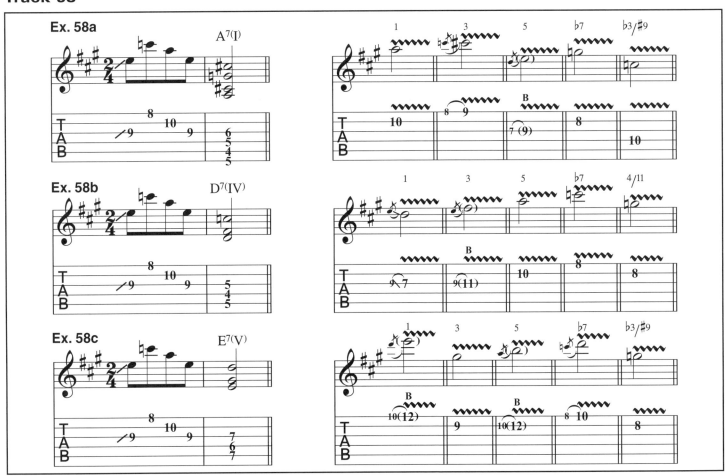

Ex. 58b

Ex. 58c

CHAPTER 6

FIVE-NOTE PICKUP LICKS

Rhythmically, each lick in our line of five-note pickups is notated in 3/8 using four consecutive sixteenth notes followed by one eighth note. And yes, these too can be personally customized with a host of 3/8 and 2/4 options from our "Rhythmic Variations" division. (See Examples 114a–h and 115a–h.)

On the disc: Once again, the "a," "b," and "c" segments of each 3/8 example have been combined on a single track. (Keep in mind that all of these five-note pickup modules were designed to begin on beat *four* when applied to a measure of 12/8.) Here's how it works: A three-beat countoff, with each dotted-quarter beat containing three eighth notes, precedes the "a" lick played into the I chord, which establishes its tonality. This is immediately followed by the same lick played into each I-chord target tone. Then the same process is repeated—minus the three-beat countoff—in time and without interruption for the "b" and "c" examples using the IV- and V-chords (*D7* and *E7*) and their respective target tones.

Track 59

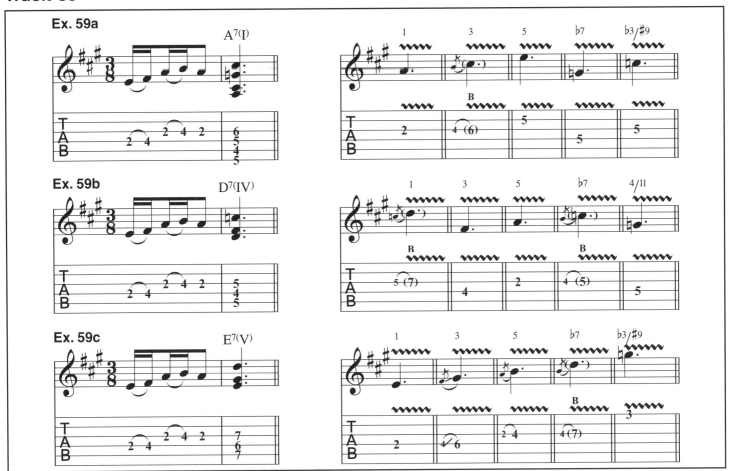

Track 60

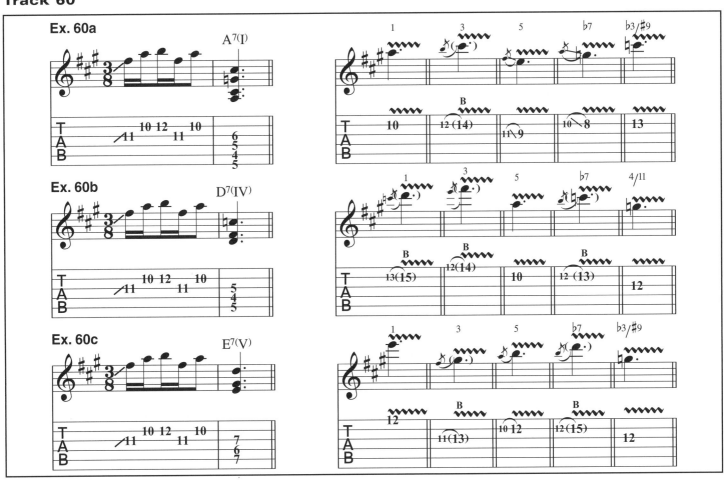

Track 61

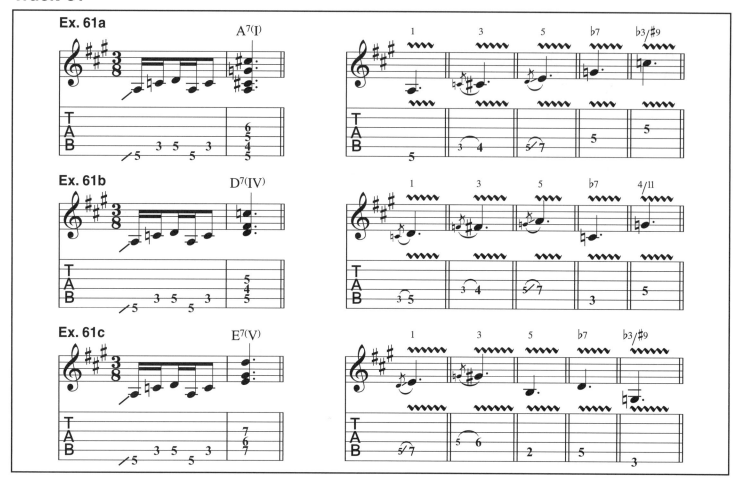

Track 62

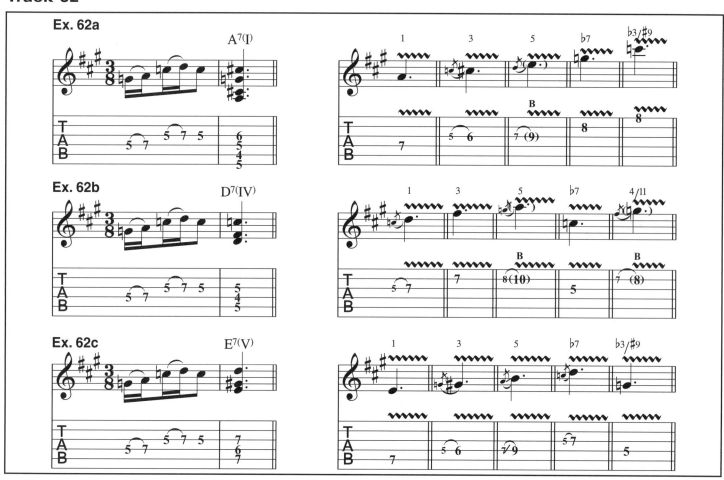

Track 63

Ex. 63a

Ex. 63b

Ex. 63c

Track 64

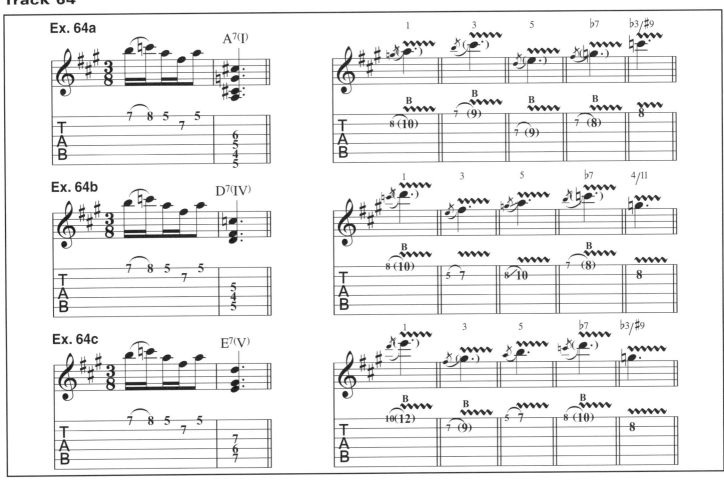

Ex. 64a

Ex. 64b

Ex. 64c

Track 65

Ex. 65a

Ex. 65b

Ex. 65c

Track 66

Ex. 66a

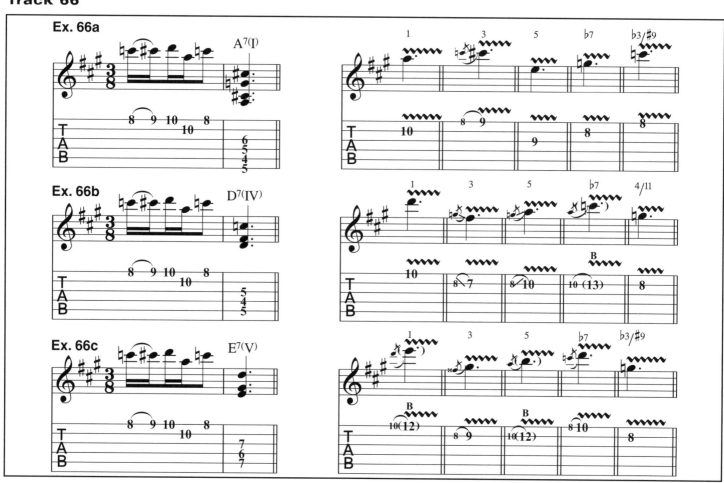

Ex. 66b

Ex. 66c

Track 67

Ex. 67a

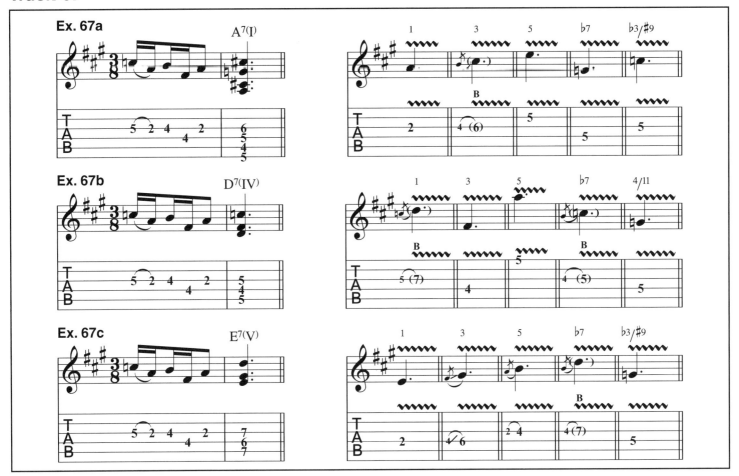

Ex. 67b

Ex. 67c

Track 68

Ex. 68a

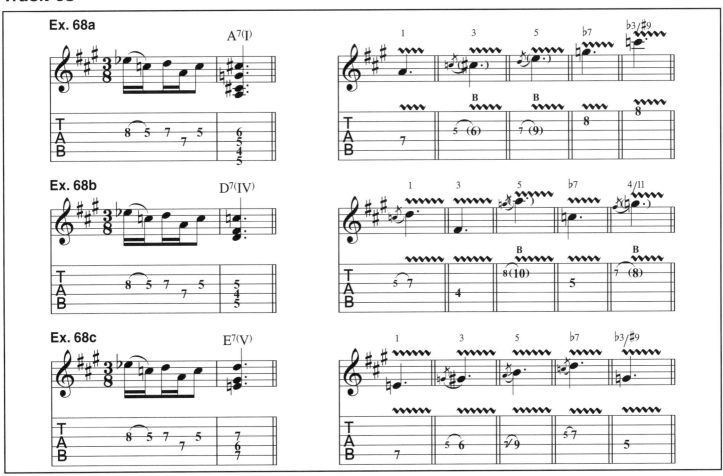

Ex. 68b

Ex. 68c

Track 69

Ex. 69a

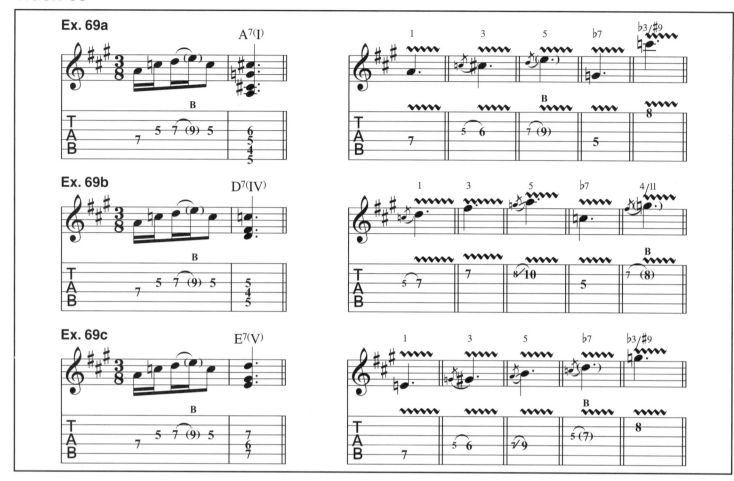

Track 70

Ex. 70a

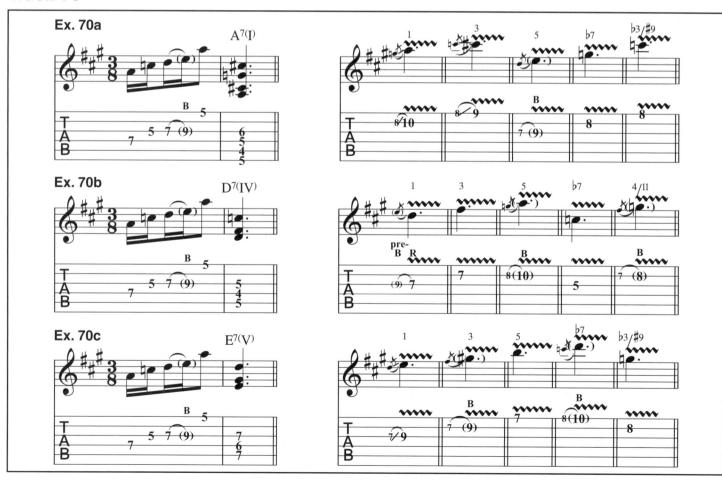

Track 71

Ex. 71a

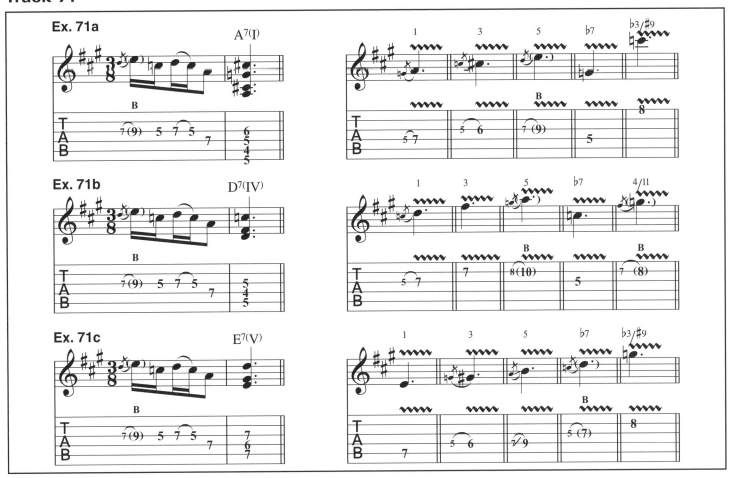

Track 72

Ex. 72a

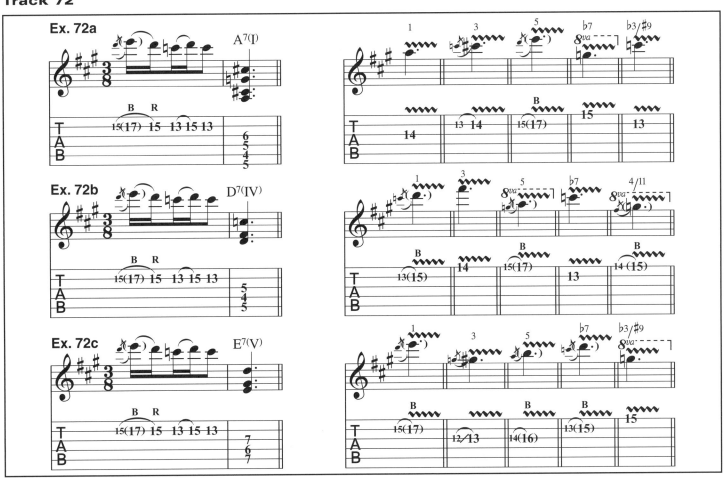

Track 73

Ex. 73a

Ex. 73b

Ex. 73c

Track 74

Ex. 74a

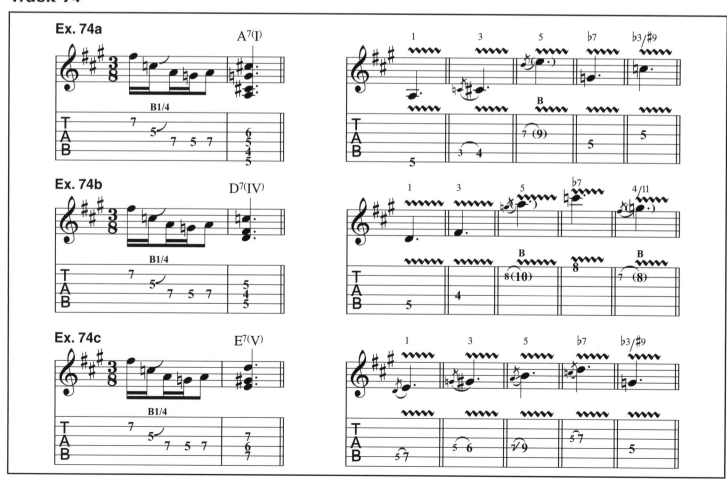

Ex. 74b

Ex. 74c

Track 75

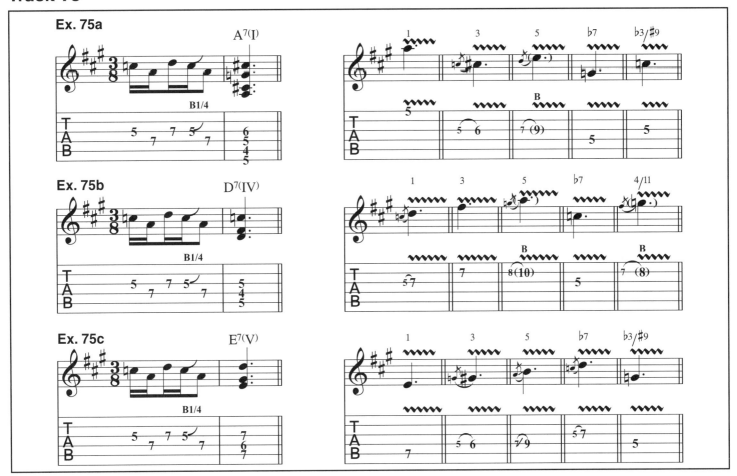

Track 76

Track 77

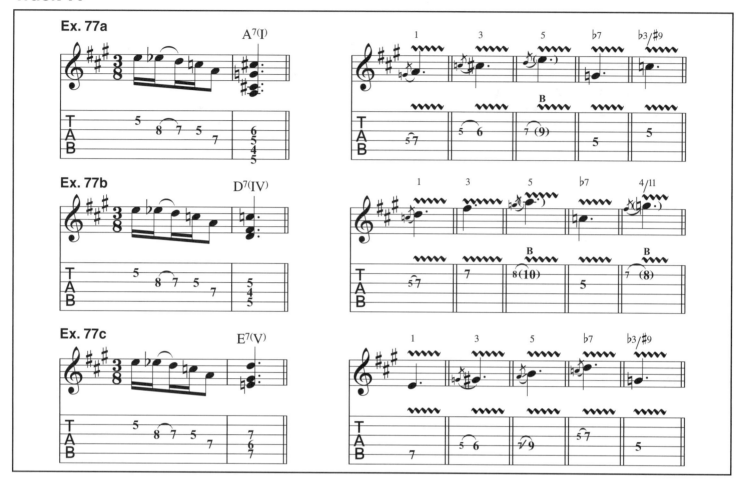

Track 78

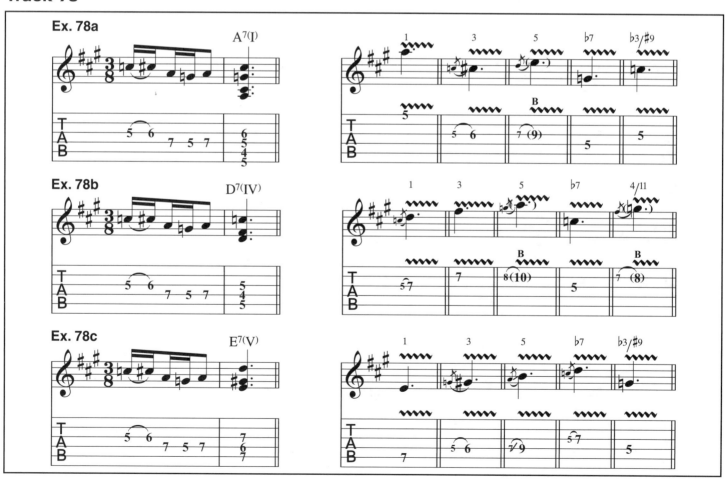

Track 79

Ex. 79a

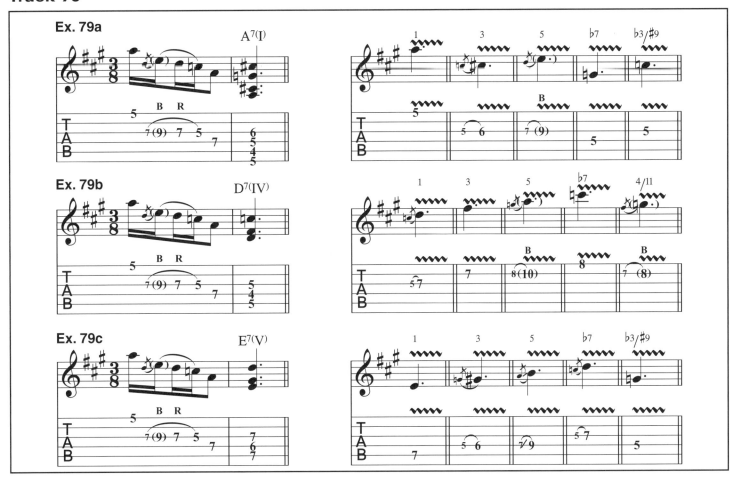

Track 80

Ex. 80a

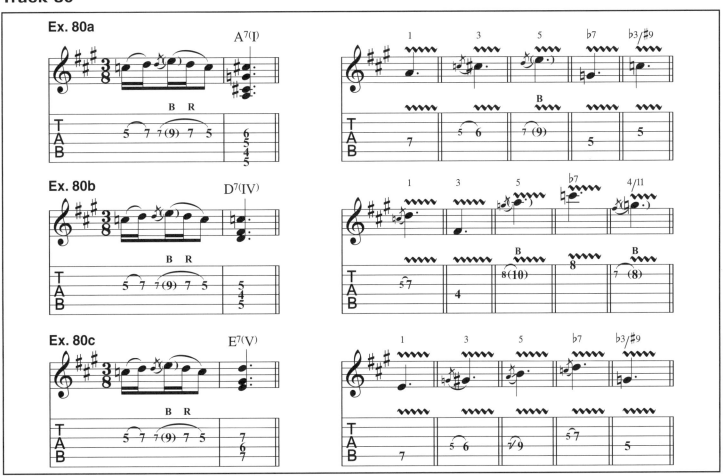

Track 81

Ex. 81a

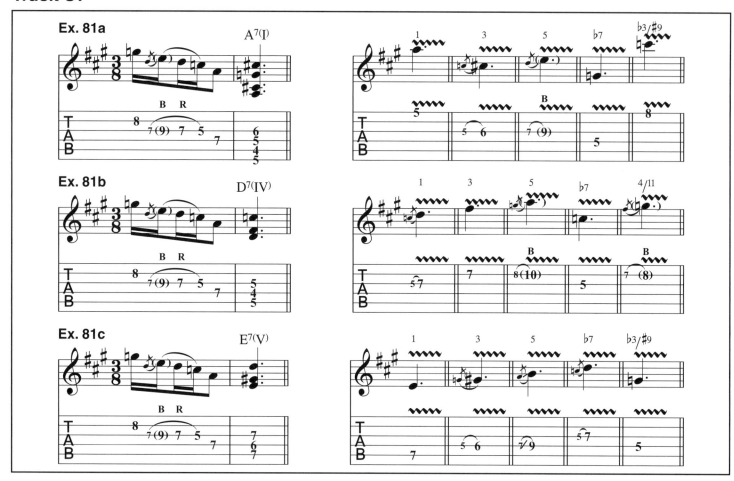

Ex. 81b

Ex. 81c

Track 82

Ex. 82a

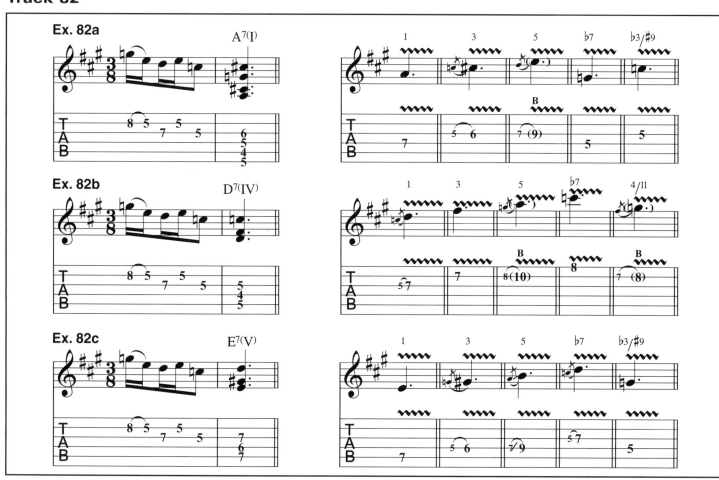

Ex. 82b

Ex. 82c

Track 83

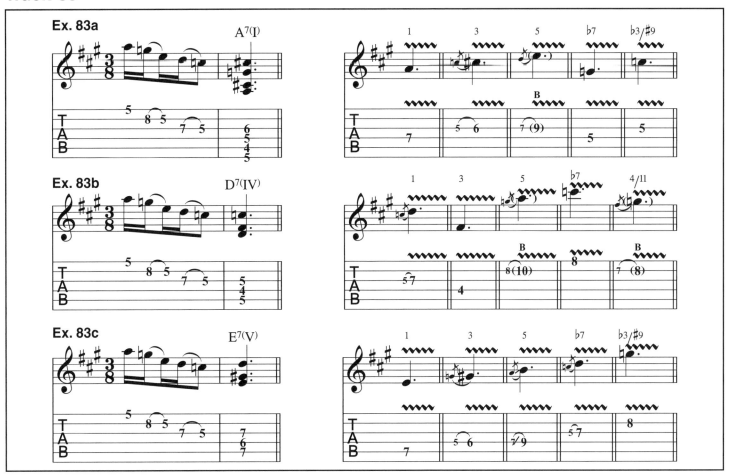

Track 84

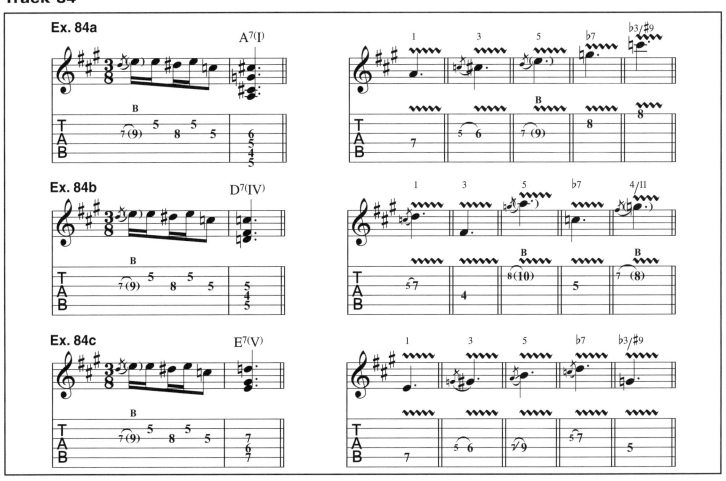

Track 85

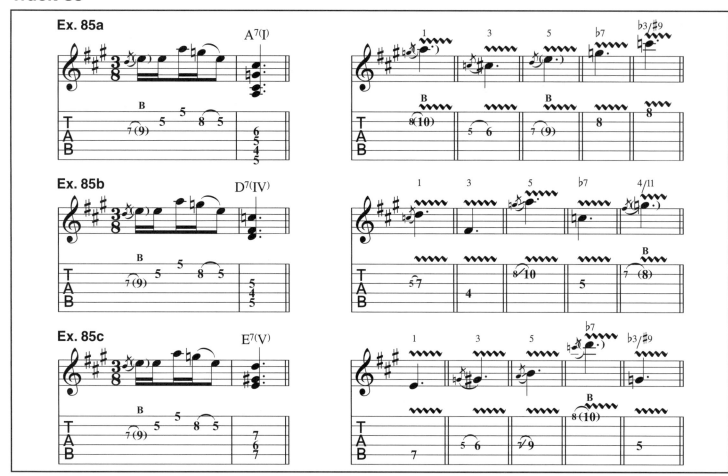

Ex. 85a

Ex. 85b

Ex. 85c

Track 86

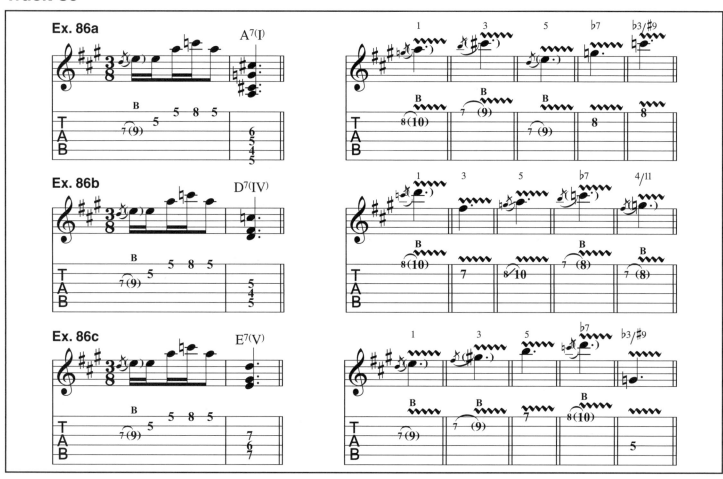

Ex. 86a

Ex. 86b

Ex. 86c

Track 87

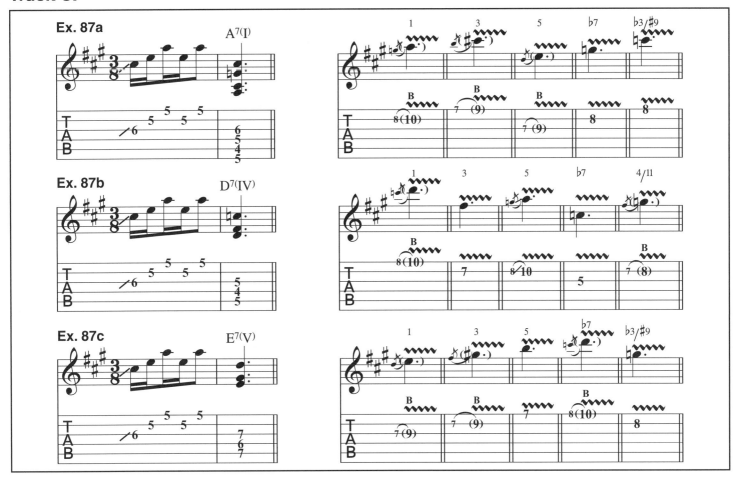

Track 88

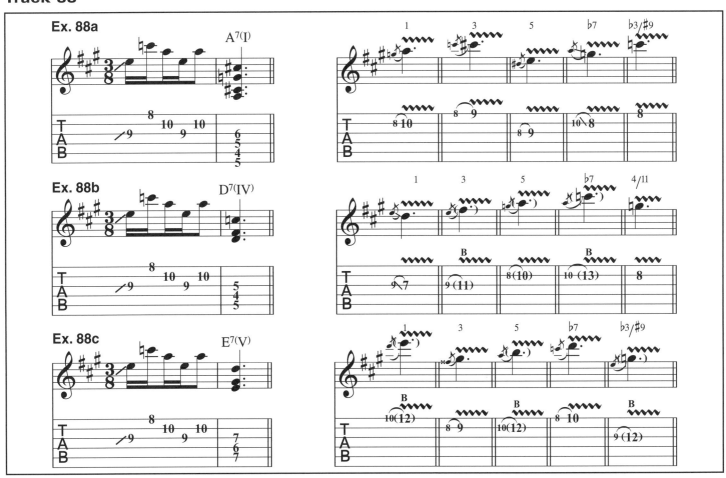

Track 89

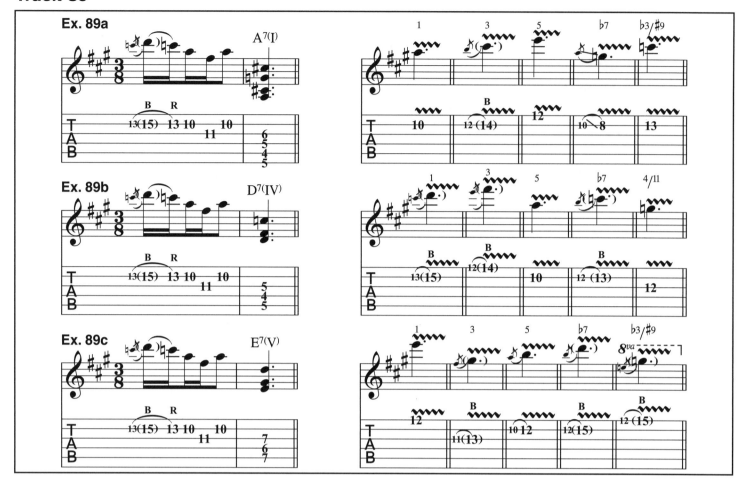

CHAPTER 7

SIX-NOTE PICKUP LICKS

Finally, each lick in our line of six-note pickups is notated in 3/8 using six consecutive sixteenth notes. (Whew! Try saying that one ten times in a row. You could even adapt its rhythm to an eight-note module.) Due to the increased amount of notes in these licks, our "Rhythmic Variations" division offers more six-note 3/8 and 2/4 options than for any other modules. (See Examples 116a–h through 118a–h.)

On the disc: Okay, for the last time, the "a," "b," and "c" segments of each 3/8 example have been combined on a single track. (Keep in mind that all of these six-note pickup modules were designed to begin on beat *four* when applied to a measure of 12/8.) Here's how it works: A three-beat countoff, with each dotted quarter beat containing three eighth notes, precedes the "a" lick played into the I chord, which establishes its tonality. This is immediately followed by the same lick played into each I-chord target tone. Then the same process is repeated—minus the three-beat countoff—in time and without interruption for the "b" and "c" examples using the IV- and V-chords (*D7* and *E7*) and their respective target tones.

Track 90

Ex. 90a

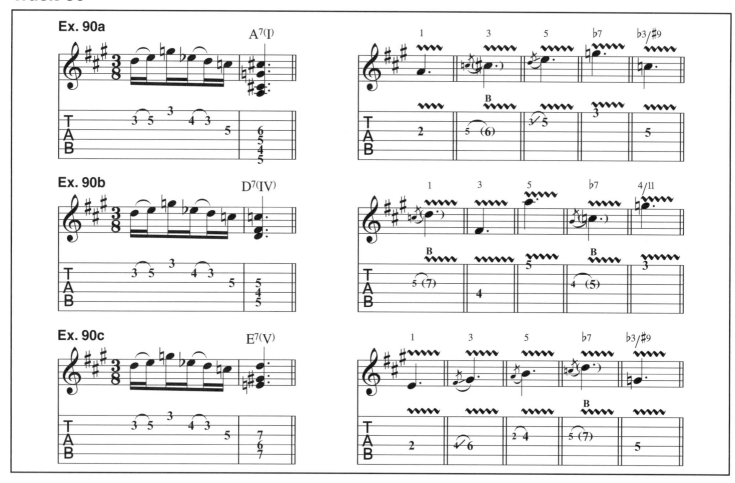

Ex. 90b

Ex. 90c

Track 91

Ex. 91a

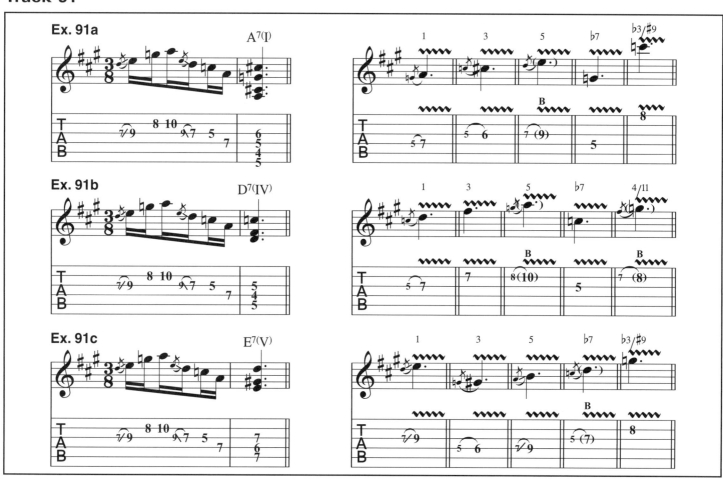

Ex. 91b

Ex. 91c

Track 92

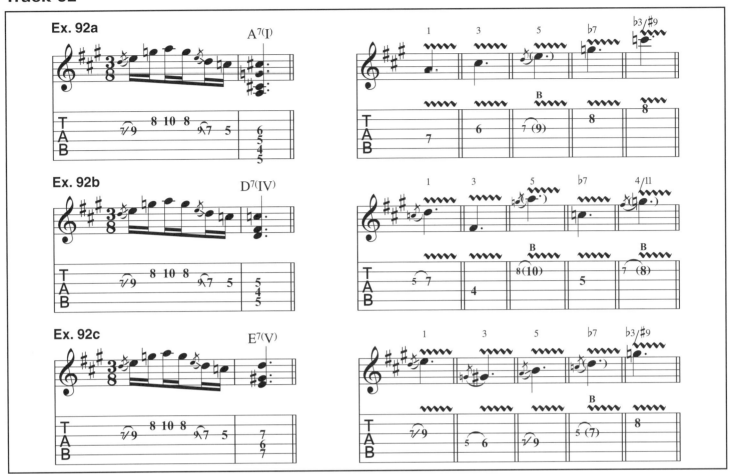

Track 93

Track 94

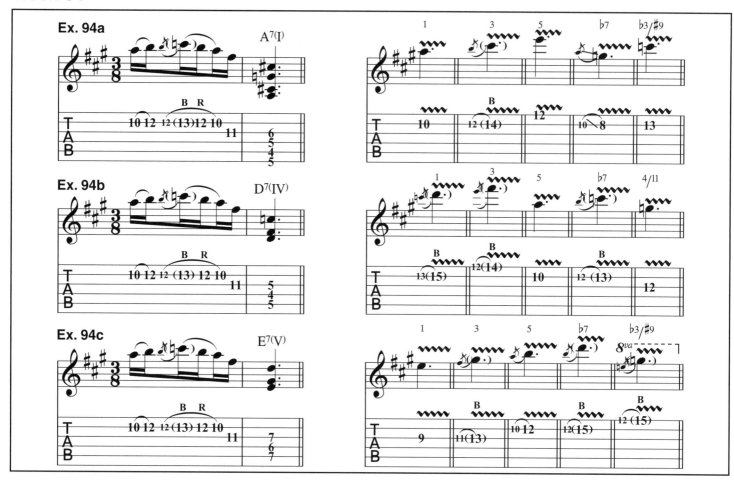

Track 95

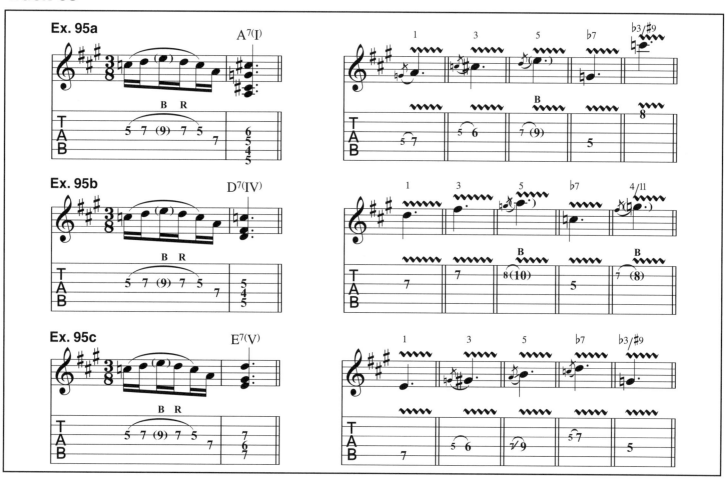

Track 96

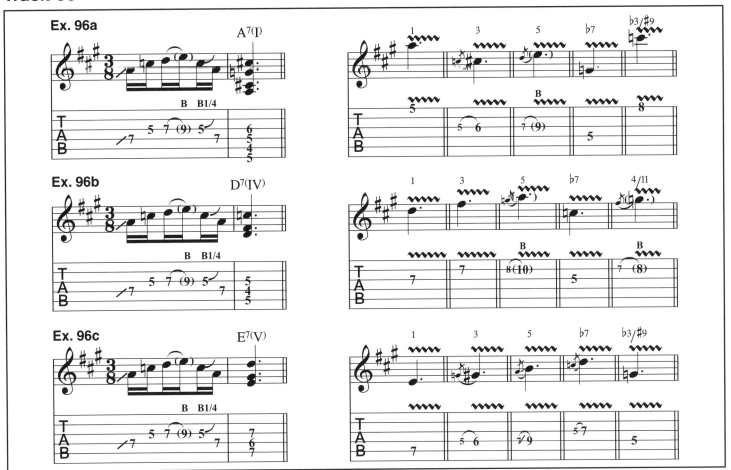

Track 97

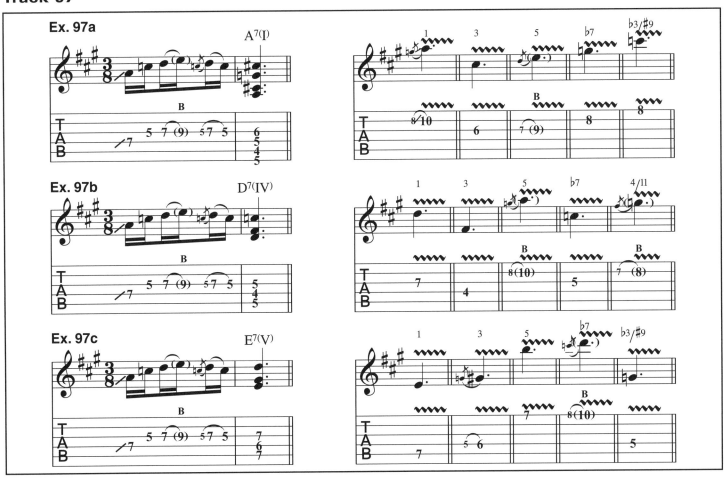

Track 98

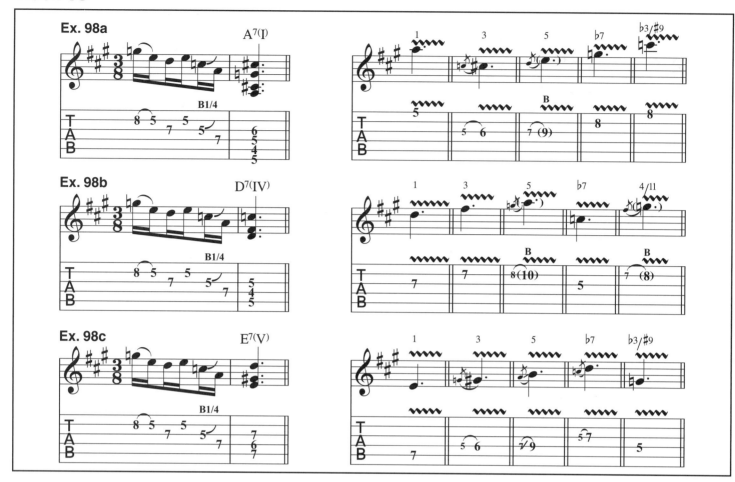

Track 99

Track 100

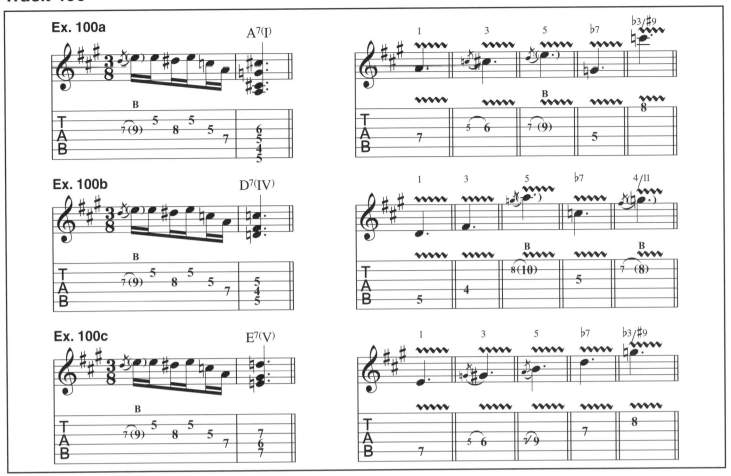

Ex. 100a

Ex. 100b

Ex. 100c

Track 101

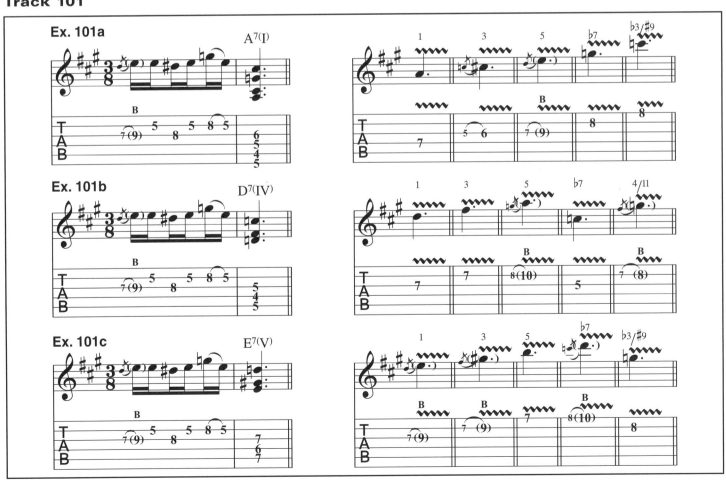

Ex. 101a

Ex. 101b

Ex. 101c

Track 102

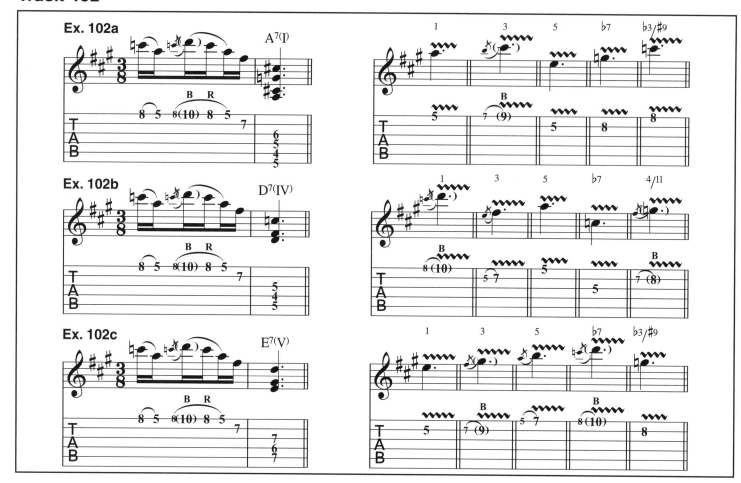

Track 103

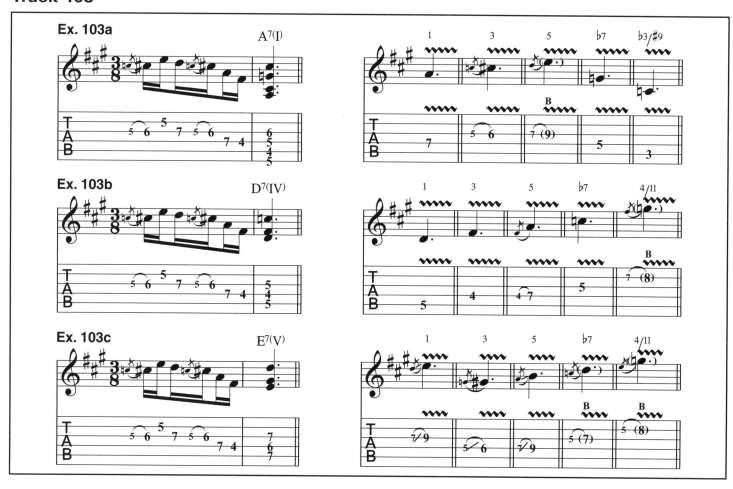

Track 104

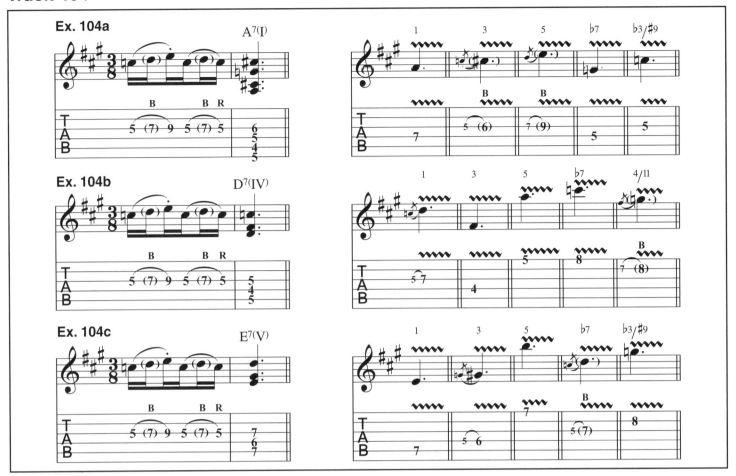

Track 105

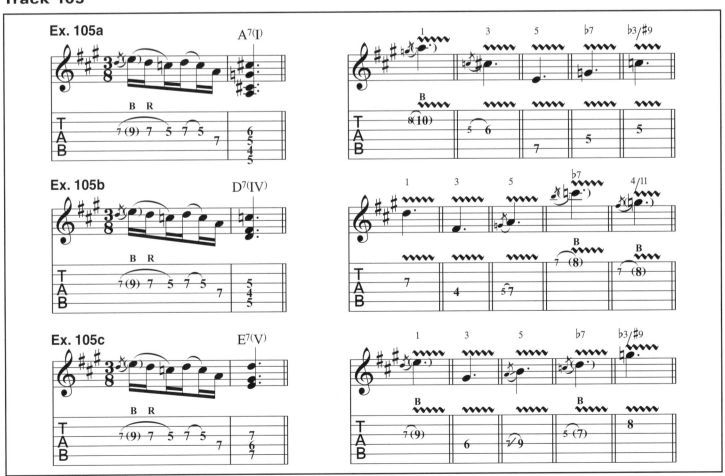

Track 106

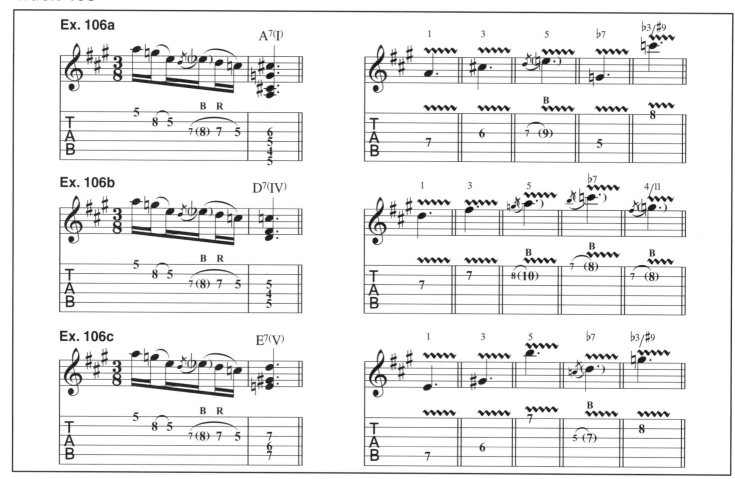

Track 107

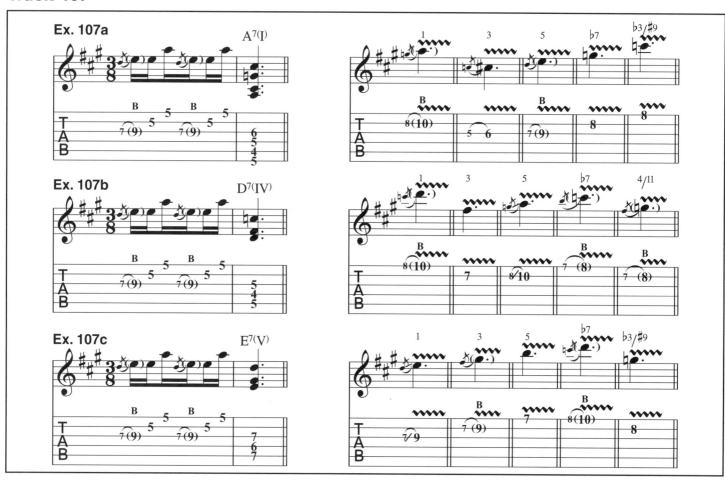

Track 108

Ex. 108a

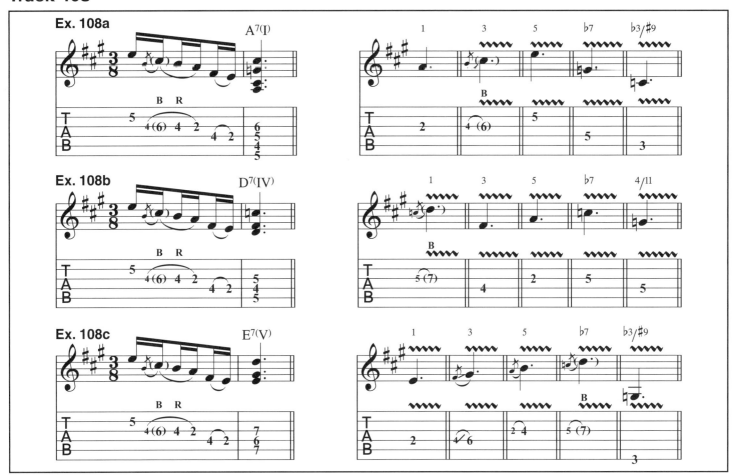

Track 109

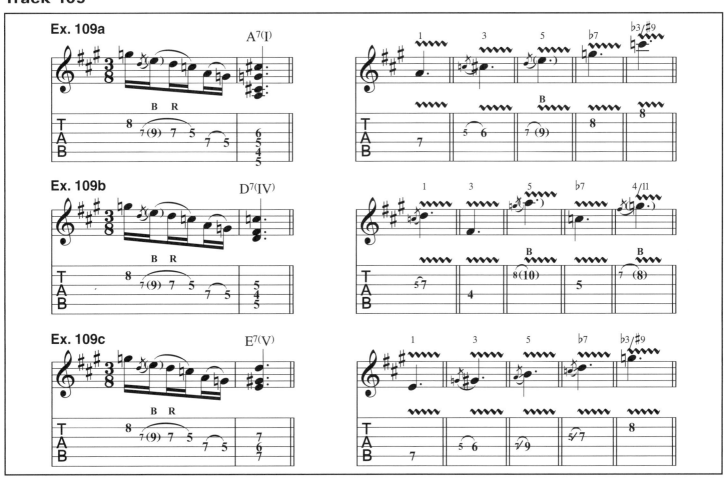

Now it's time to let the cat out of the bag: Though the previous 109 three-, four-, five- and six-note examples have been presented as pickup licks designed to begin on beat *four* in 12/8 and beat *three* in 4/4, the truth is you can start all of them on any beat you choose —just be sure to target the chord of the moment.

CHAPTER 8

RHYTHMIC VARIATIONS

Rhythmically, we've notated all of our three-, four-, five-, and six-note lick modules in as compact a manner as possible. This makes them easy to read, retain, and recall, but unfortunately limits their diversity. (This mainly applies to our straight eighth-note-based three- and four-note licks. Many of the five- and six-note licks stand on their own as written.) To help you unlock their diversity, we supply the following rhythmic options for every lick. Additionally, each one of these rhythmic variations can be half-timed or double-timed to create hundreds more. You'll find that some will work better than others, but you should try each one out with every lick and "save" the ones that tickle your fancy.

The following rhythms are written in the two metric categories that correspond with our three-, four-, five-, and six-note lick modules: 3/8 and 2/4. All rhythmic variations in each category are demonstrated using the same three-, four-, five-, or six-note lick (based on Example 1) so you can stay focused on the rhythm at hand.

On the disc: Each group of three-, four-, and five-note rhythmic variations appears on two adjacent tracks—one for 3/8 rhythms and one for 2/4 rhythms—while the six-note examples span three tracks. Following a four-beat countoff, each variation is repeated four times. The same process is repeated for each consecutively lettered example. You can cue forward or backward and use the space between each rhythmic variation to locate a desired track. If this becomes too cumbersome, try burning each lettered example to CD as a separate track.

Track 110

Track 111

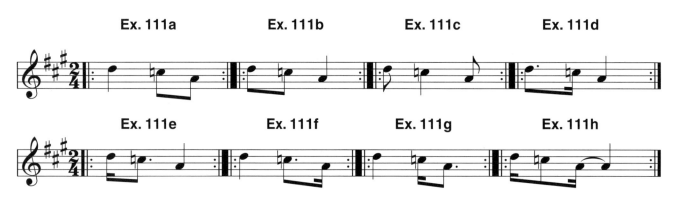

Track 112

Track 113

Ex. 113a   Ex. 113b   Ex. 113c   Ex. 113d

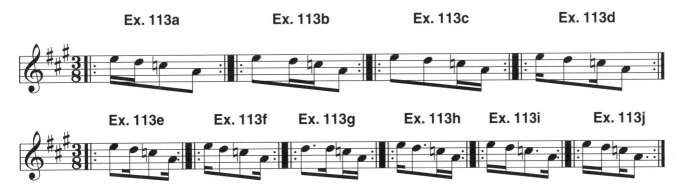

Ex. 113e   Ex. 113f   Ex. 113g   Ex. 113h   Ex. 113i   Ex. 113j

Track 114

Ex. 114a   Ex. 114b   Ex. 114c   Ex. 114d

Ex. 114e   Ex. 114f   Ex. 114g   Ex. 114h

Track 115

Ex. 115a   Ex. 115b   Ex. 115c   Ex. 115d

Ex. 115e   Ex. 115f   Ex. 115g   Ex. 115h

Track 116

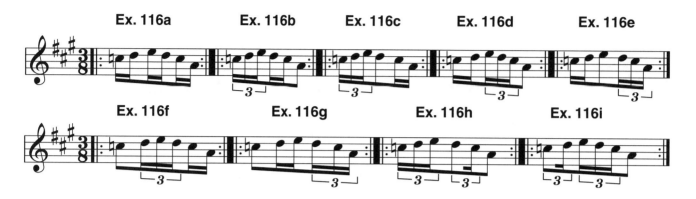

Ex. 116a   Ex. 116b   Ex. 116c   Ex. 116d   Ex. 116e

Ex. 116f   Ex. 116g   Ex. 116h   Ex. 116i

Track 117

Ex. 117a   Ex. 117b   Ex. 117c   Ex. 117d

Ex. 117e   Ex. 117f   Ex. 117g   Ex. 117h

Track 118

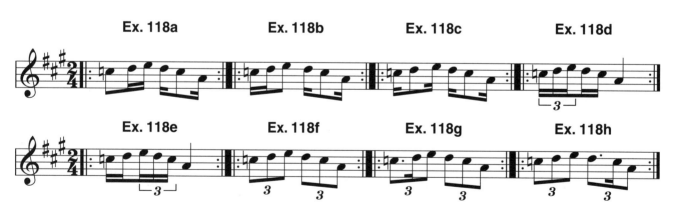

Ex. 118a   Ex. 118b   Ex. 118c   Ex. 118d

Ex. 118e   Ex. 118f   Ex. 118g   Ex. 118h

CHAPTER 9

ONE-BAR TARGET-TONE BLUES LICKS

Whew! With all that target practice under your belt, you may be wondering what to do *after* you hit the bull's-eye. That's precisely why we manufacture this custom line of one-bar target-tone licks: Each of the following 84 multifunctional licks begins and, in most cases, ends on one of the nine target tones in the key of *A* (although ending on the same note is certainly not a rule). These are designed to fasten directly to the three-, four-, five-, and six-note lick modules in Examples 1–109, and may be dropped into any appropriate measure in a standard quick-change or slow-change 12-bar blues progression. Slick, eh? We also supply choice applications for each group of licks, both in the introduction to each target tone—where the tone-of-the-moment is analyzed against *A7* (I), *D7* (IV), and *E7* (V)—as well as above every music example. The licks are presented in paired "a" and "b" examples on the CD. Two licks are heard on each track, and each one is preceded by a one-bar 12/8 countoff. Since there are several applications for each lick, it's up to you to define the chord-of-the-moment. (I recommend sounding the chord you choose just before playing the lick in order to attune your ear to its harmonic environment.)

So dig back into the depths of the first 109 examples, mine all of your favorite pickup modules, and weld them to these hip one-bar blues moves.

On the disc: Each audio track contains the "a" and "b" sections of each example separated by a four-beat countoff. Short 'n' sweet.

A TARGET LICKS

Applications: *A* = 1 (root) of *A7* (I); 5 of *D7* (IV)

Option: *A* = 4/11 of *E7* (V)

Targeting the tonic *A*, the first five two-part examples are typical I-chord runs that can be dropped directly into bars 1, 3, 4, 7, 8, or 11 of any standard 12-bar blues progression (add bar 2 during slow-change progressions). The commonality between chord tones and omission of *C#* enables you to play Examples 119a&b, 120b, 121b, 122a&b, and 123a&b over any chord in the progression, so you may also insert these examples into bars 2, 5, 6, or 10 over *D7* (omit bar 2 during slow-change progressions), and bars 9 or 12 over *E7*. Let your ears tell you which applications work best.

Track 119

Ex. 119a   **Ex. 119b**

Track 120

Ex. 120a   **Ex. 120b**

Track 121

Ex. 121a   **Ex. 121b**

Track 122

Ex. 122a   **Ex. 122b**

Track 123

Ex. 123a   **Ex. 123b**

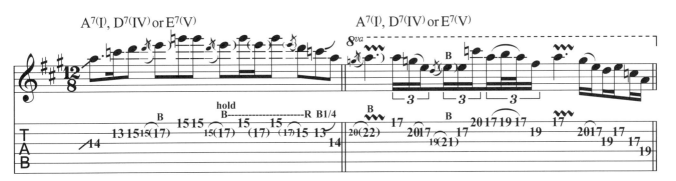

C TARGET LICKS

Applications: $C = \flat3/\sharp9$ of $A7$ (I); $\flat7$ of $D7$ (IV)

Option: $C = \sharp5/\flat6$ of $E7$ (V)

The next five paired examples begin on C, one of the tangiest target tones in the A blues tonality. They make ideal IV-chord licks when played over bars 2, 5, 6, and 10 (omit bar 2 during slow-change progressions), but can also venture into $A7$ and $E7$ territory, again due to common chord tones and extensions. The lone exception is Example129b, which was designed for IV-chord use only. (Tip: C is one of your best wild cards for creating altered tension over $A7$ in bars 1, 3, 4, 7, 8, or 11 [add bar 2 during slow-change progressions], where it functions as the $\flat3/\sharp9$, and $E7$ in bars 9 or 12, where it serves as the $\sharp5$.)

Track 124

Ex. 124a

Ex. 124b

Track 125

Ex. 125a

Ex. 125b

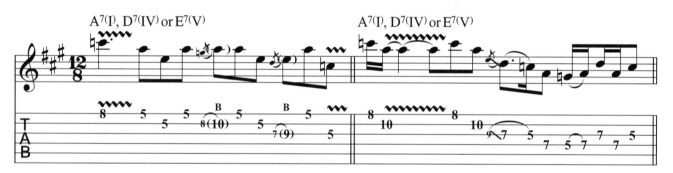

Track 126

Ex. 126a

Ex. 126b

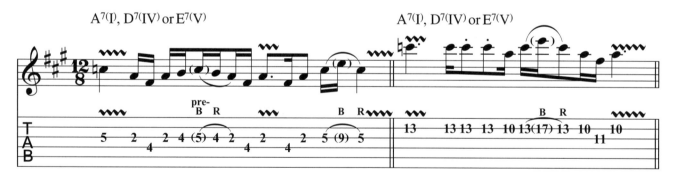

Track 127

Ex. 127a

Ex. 127b

Track 128

Ex. 128a

Ex. 128b

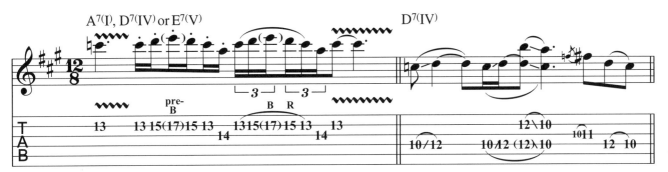

C# TARGET LICKS

Application: *C# = 3 of A7* (I)

Option: *C# = 6/13 of E7* (V)

Essentially, the *C#* target tone that begins the next five multipart examples limits their usage to the I (*A7*) chord in bars 1, 3, 4, 7, 8, or 10 of a 12-bar quick-change blues progression. (Add bar 2 during slow-change progressions.) New...no, make that Old Rule: *Never* target *C#* on the downbeats in any measure containing *D7*; it's the natural 7 of the chord and one of the sourest tones you can target. The only appropriate application of *C#* to this IV chord is as a passing tone placed on a weak beat, such as a succession of *C–C#–D* or *D–C#–C* eighth notes. (See Examples 29b, 30b, and 158b.) However, it is possible to cleverly work it into an *E7* lick during bars 9 or 12, as you'll soon discover in Example 132a, the only example in the lot tailored to the V chord.

Track 129

Ex. 129a

Ex. 129b

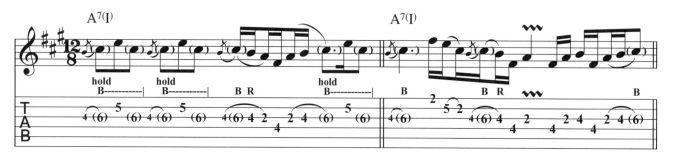

Track 130

Ex. 130a

Ex. 130b

Track 131

Ex. 131a

Ex. 131b

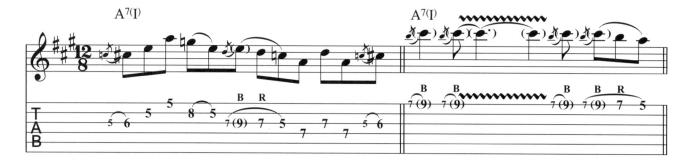

Track 132

Ex. 132a   **Ex. 132b**

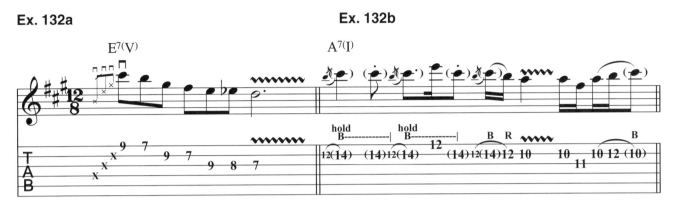

Track 133

Ex. 133a   **Ex. 133b**

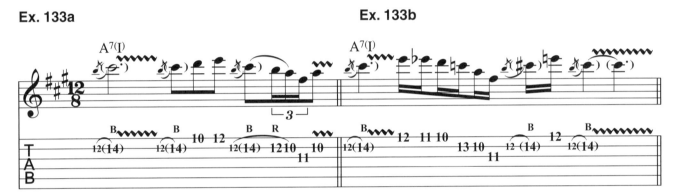

D TARGET LICKS

Applications: *D* = 1 (root) of *D7* (IV); ♭7 of *E7* (V)

Option: *D* = 4/11 of *A7* (I)

Targeting *D*, as we do in the next ten licks, works well if you're aiming for *D7* (bars 2, 5, 6, or 10—omit bar 2 during slow-change progressions) or *E7* (bars 9 or 12), but the fact that the note is the 4/11 of *A7* creates a suspended, unsettled vibe over the I chord that begs for resolution, usually to *C#, C*, or *E*. Examples 134a&b, 136a and 137a work for both *D7 and E7*, while Examples 135b, 136b, and 138b were designed for *D7* only, and Example 135a is tailored to fit *E7*. Finally Examples 137b and 138a will accommodate any chord in the 12-bar progression.

Track 134

Ex. 134a

Ex. 134b

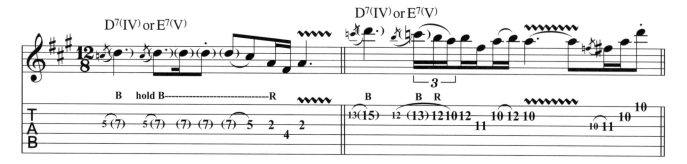

Track 135

Ex. 135a

Ex. 135b

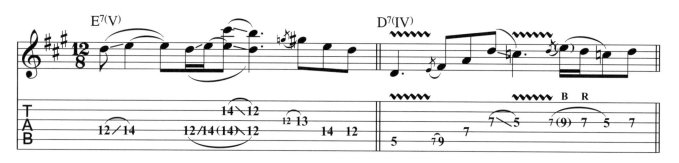

Track 136

Ex. 136a

Ex. 136b

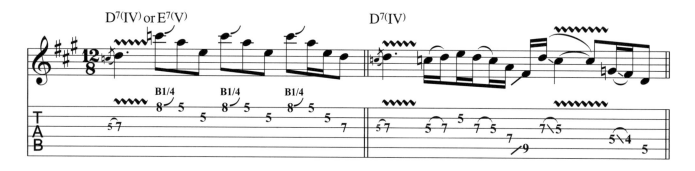

Track 137

Ex. 137a   **Ex. 137b**

Track 138

Ex. 138a   **Ex. 138b**

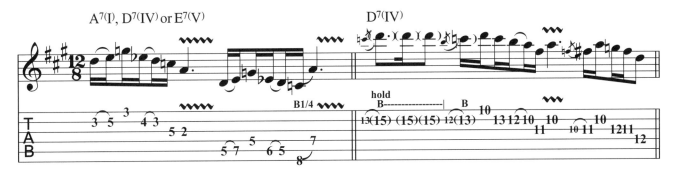

E TARGET LICKS

Applications: *E* = 5 of *A7* (I); 1(root) of *E7* (IV)

Option: *E* = 2/9 of *D7* (IV)

An *E* target tone common to both *A7* and *E7*, as well as a tasty extension of *D7*, kicks off the next batch of licks, which come on strong in all three applications. You can drop any of these examples into literally any measure of a 12-bar quick-change or slow-change blues progression. No rules!

Track 139

Ex. 139a

Ex. 139b

Track 140

Ex. 140a

Ex. 140b

Track 141

Ex. 141a

Ex. 141b

Track 142

Ex. 142a

Ex. 142b

Track 143

Ex. 143a

Ex. 143b

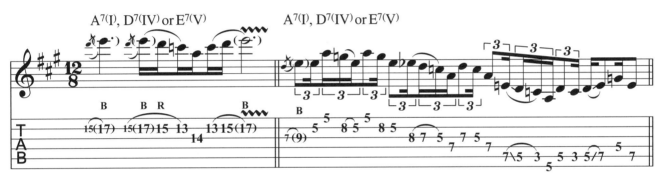

F# TARGET LICKS

Application: *F# = 3 of D7 (IV)*

Options: *F# = 6 of A7 (I); 2/9 of E7 (V)*

Being cast as the 3 of *D7* makes *F#* a surefire ingredient for cooking up some tasty IV-chord licks. The proof is in the pudding: Examples 144a&b–147a will spice up your *D7* chords in bars 2, 5, 6, or 10 (omit bar 2 during slow-change progressions), while Example 147b was specifically molded to enhance *A7* (you know the measure numbers by now, right?), although you could also get away with using it to season *E7* in bars 9 or 12. Examples 14a&b present a pair of globally correct licks that complement the flavor of all three chords, so you can use them anywhere in the 12-bar progression. Simmer and season to taste.

Track 144

Ex. 144a

Ex. 144b

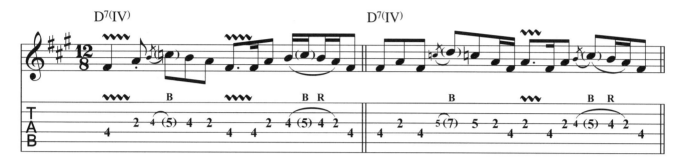

Track 145

Ex. 145a

Ex. 145b

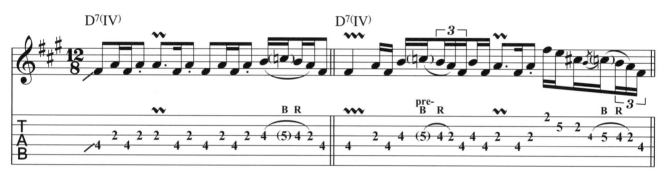

Track 146

Ex. 146a

Ex. 146b

Track 147

Ex. 147a   **Ex. 147b**

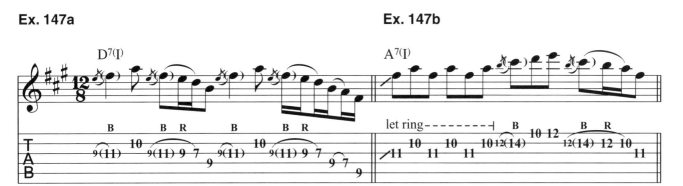

Track 148

Ex. 148a   **Ex. 148b**

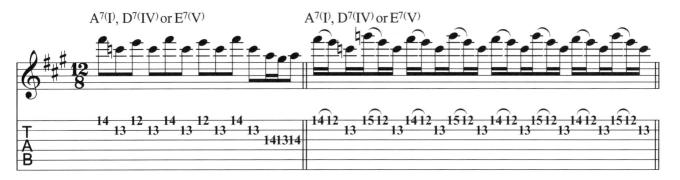

G TARGET LICKS

Application: $G = \flat 7$ of A7(I)

Options: G = 4/11 of D7(IV); $\flat 3/\#9$ of E7(V)

G is another particularly juicy target tone that sits comfortably with all three chords. Hence, with the exception of Examples 149a and 150a, which are tailored to A7, the following ten one-bar moves get along equally well with A7, D7, and E7. Drop 'em wherever you please.

Track 149

Ex. 149a

Ex. 149b

Track 150

Ex. 150a

Ex. 150b

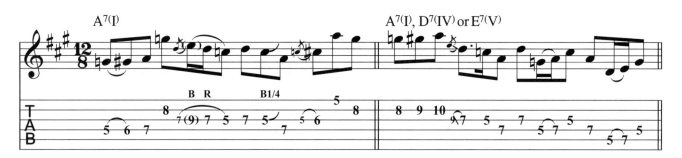

Track 151

Ex. 151a

Ex. 151b

Track 152

Ex. 152a

Ex. 152b

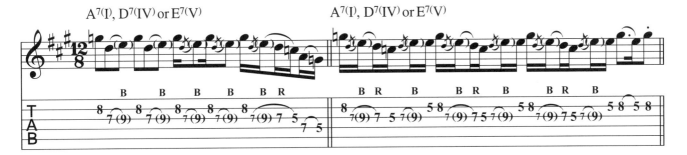

Track 153

Ex. 153a

Ex. 153b

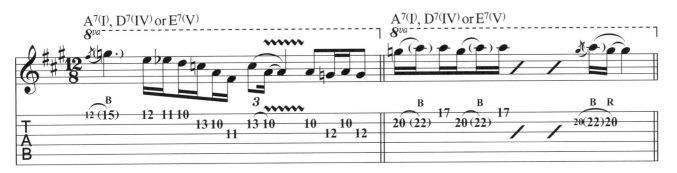

G# TARGET LICKS

Application: *G# = 3 of E7 (V)*

Options: = See below.

As the 3 of the V chord, *G#* is an ideal choice for kicking off an *E7* target tone lick, but be careful: Like *C#* against *D7*, applying *G#* to *A7* or *D7* requires special care due to the fact that it is the 7 of the I chord and the b5 of the IV chord. Once again, if you want to tread onto I- or IV-chord turf with this tone, your best approach is to insert *G#* on a weak beat between *G* and *A* so that it operates as a passing tone. Go back to Examples 27a&b and 28a&b, or check out bar 7 in Blues Solo #3 (Example 187) to hear this concept in action.

Track 154

Ex. 154a

Ex. 154b

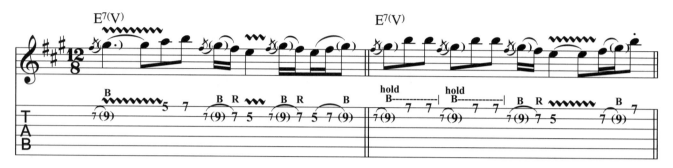

Track 155

Ex. 155a

Ex. 155b

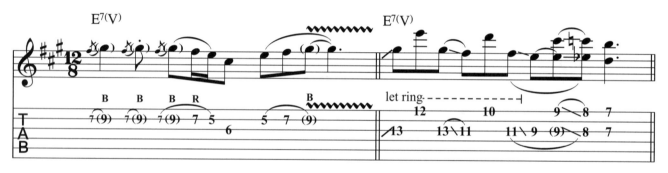

Track 156

Ex. 156a

Ex. 156b

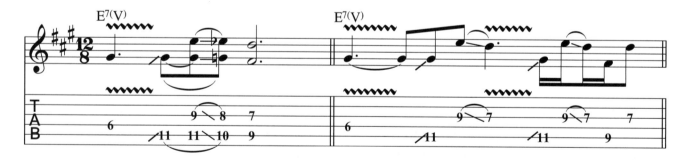

B TARGET LICKS

Application: *B* = 5 of *E7* (V)

Options: *B* = 2/9 of *A7* (I); 6/13 of *D7* (IV)

Our last group of target tone licks start on *B*, the 5 of *E7* and an obvious electorate for V-chord licks in bars 9 or 12. While it's technically correct, the results of this choice of target are often less than tantalizing and even disappointing due to its own incongruity. So as to not end on a bum note, we'll attempt to remedy the situation with the last eight licks in this section. Here's the lineup: Examples 157a&b, 158a, and 159a&b are V-chord/*E7* licks, and Example 158b is strictly for IV-chord/*D7* usage, while Example 160a can be applied to both. (You know the bar numbers.) Finally, in a show of peace and goodwill, Example 160 lovingly communes with all three chords.

Track 157

Ex. 157a   **Ex. 157b**

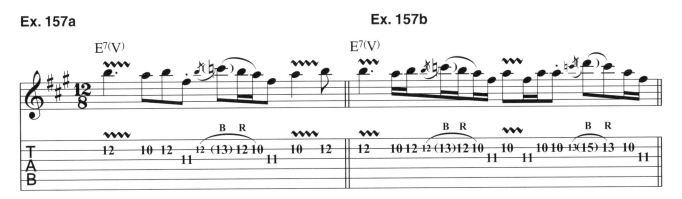

Track 158

Ex. 158a   **Ex. 158b**

103

Track 159

Ex. 159a

Ex. 159b

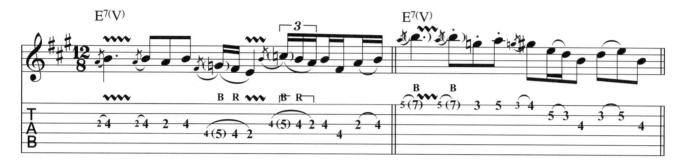

Track 160

Ex. 160a

Ex. 160b

CHAPTER 10

TWO-BAR BLUES LICKS

I t's time to double your pleasure. The following licks were conceived to fit into specific two-bar segments within a standard 12-bar blues progression in the key of A—we'll favor the quick-change version unless otherwise indicated—but once again the commonality of some chord tones makes them multifunctional, and that's a beautiful thing. These licks illustrate how to play into, over, and across each chord change in the progression. A short analysis precedes each example in order to demonstrate how many of the previous modular and target-tone licks have been conjoined, altered, or otherwise permuted.

On the disc: Each two-bar lick gets its own audio track. 'Nuff said.

I-CHORD LICKS

The first two examples are static I (*A7*) chord runs designed to fit snugly into bars 3 and 4, or 7 and 8, plus bars 1 and 2, or 11 and 12, during slow-change progressions.

Example 161 kicks off with a one-bar, two-against-three lick comprised of alternating 5's (*E*) and ♭7's (*G*). Finger both notes simultaneously, speed up the tempo, and you've got a pretty convincing harmonica riff. (Tip: Use your neck pickup with the tone control rolled back and some tube-amp overdrive to reinforce this vibe.) Notice how this melodic scheme causes these two notes to reverse positions in each successive triplet. You can apply this type of melodic and rhythmic displacement to any two notes. The *A* root is introduced in bar 2 before we ride the *G* string down to the third position for some hearty riffing that includes a bluesy bent-and-released ♭5 (*Eb*) passing tone. The absence of *C#* and abundance of common chord tones and extensions throughout this lick also make it an ideal choice for both the IV (*D7*) chord and V (*E7*) chords.

Track 161

Ex. 161

Conversely, Example 162 zeroes in on the *3/C#*, which ties it to the *A* pentatonic major scale and totally jives with *A7*, but also limits its usage to the I chord. Lock into the eighth position, reinforce your third finger, and have at these sweet-as-honey sustained melodic bends and releases. Don't forget the staccato dots, and, as always, work that vibrato! Note how the variance between rhythms in bars 1 and 2 creates a cool, conversational question-and-answer type of flow. (Tip: Drop all *C#* bends one half-step to *C*, and you can milk this lick over *D7* or *E7* till the cows come home.)

Track 162

Ex. 162

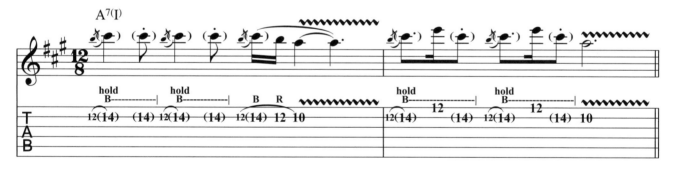

I–IV LICKS

The next two licks raise a pair of possibilities for navigating the I–IV (*A7–D7*) change that occurs between bars 1 and 2 and bars 4 and 5 during a quick-change 12-bar blues progression.

Beginning with a grace-hammered ♭3–3 target that screams "*A7*," Example 163 snakes through some standard blues-approved middle-register licks derived from the fifth-position *A* pentatonic minor "blues box," a pet moniker given to the most commonly used *A* pentatonic minor/blues scale pattern. The *C* on the downbeat of bar 2 nails the *D7*, as does the following organ-like riff that alternates pedal *A* tones with fifth- and seventh-fret double stops on the *B* and *G* strings.

Track 163

Ex. 163

Example 164 borrows the opening of Example 161, transposes it up one octave to the fifteenth fret, and converts it to a nifty bent-and-held-5-to-stationary-♭7 move. The third bend is held, then released as a picked grace note, and the double-timed repetitive *F#–E–C* motif that follows in bar 2—you may remember this move from Examples 148a and 148b—defines the IV/*D7* chord in conjunction with the bend to high *A* and double-timed variation of this example's opening motif. Again, the lack of *C#* makes this lick open game for any chord in the progression.

Track 164

Ex. 164

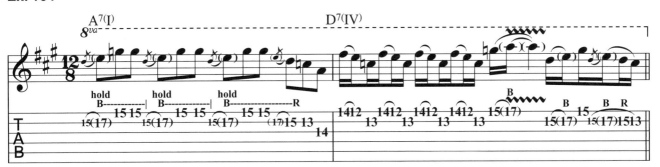

IV–I LICKS

Logically, the next two licks cover the IV–I (*D7–A7*) change that occurs between bars 2 and 3 and bars 10 and 11 during a quick-change 12-bar blues progression. Tack these, or your own adaptations, onto the end of both previous examples to form a four-bar I–IV–IV–I phrase suitable for bars 4 through 7.

For instance, the common double stops that commence Example 165 could easily be connected directly to the end of Example 163 to form a seamless four-bar *A7–D7–D7–A7* run. You may recognize the bent-and-released double stops on beat *three* of bar 1 as a favorite Chuck Berry cum T-Bone Walker lick. The spirit of T-Bone also infuses the return to the I chord in bar 2, especially in the use of the *9/B* in the hammer-on/pull-off maneuver on beat *four*. (Tip: SRV put his stamp on this move by lowering the *B* one half step to *Bb*, the ♭9.)

Track 165

Ex. 165

We've all but completely neglected to include rests in any previous licks (we want you to get your money's worth), but Example 166 shows how effective a little breathing space can be. Holding off for two eighth notes before beginning each measure creates a nice pregnant pause. We've already played most of these moves, but upping the tempo to a medium shuffle really brings this lick to life. (Tip: Replace the C# in bar 2 with C, and you can drop the entire lick into any two adjacent measures.)

Track 166

Ex. 166

I–V LICKS

Our next two examples were designed to venture across the border from I (*A7*) chord to V (*E7*) chord territory. They are typically applicable to bars 8 and 9, but can also serve as I–V turnarounds in bars 11 and 12.

Broken minor-third intervals ascend the *G* and *B* strings in bar 1 of Example 167, defining four important *A* pentatonic scale positions along the way. Notice how these shapes alternate between *A* pentatonic major patterns on beats *one* and *three* and *A* pentatonic minor/blues patterns on beats *two* and *four*. Study the whole-step, whole-step, one-and-a-half-step spacing configuration between these minor-third shapes and learn to apply this "blues matrix" to all keys. The high *E* bends, and the inclusion of *B* and *F#* in bar 2 tightly binds the second half of this run to *E7*. This is also a great example of how to directly transpose a I-chord lick to the V.

Track 167

Ex. 167

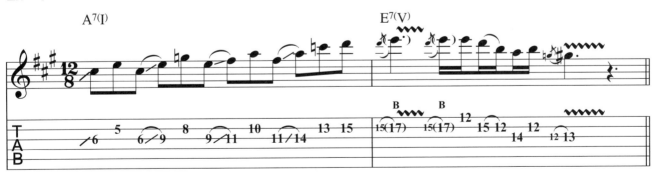

A busy, fifth-position run in bar 1 of Example 168 utilizes the bluesy ♭5 (*Eb*) and ♭3/#9 (*C*) during beat *one*, but quickly shifts back to the 5 (*E*) and 3 (*C#*) to lock in with *A7* for the remainder of the measure. Once again, a heavily emphasized *G#*—this time played using silky bends—and inclusion of *B* in bar 2 limit its multitasking abilities. (Tip: After playing this lick over bars 8 and 9, transpose bar 2 down one whole step verbatim to cover the pending IV/*D7*-chord change in bar 10.)

Track 168

Ex. 168

V–IV LICKS

Nearing the end of the 12-bar cycle, the following two licks cover the V–IV change in bars 9 and 10. While it's often possible to directly transpose an *A7* lick up three and one-half steps and use exactly the same fingering over *E7*, this doesn't always work with the V–IV change. Try playing the first measure in these examples one whole step lower in bar 2, and let your ears be the judge.

Example 169 proves that you don't have to get too busy or flashy to be effective. (Of course, this depends on your choice of tempo.) The absence of audible bend releases characterizes the mostly descending V-chord run in bar 1, while bar 2 mixes in more familiar elements. Both measures begin on *D*, albeit one octave apart. There's nary a *C#* or *G#* in sight, so feel free to drop this lick bomb anywhere.

Track 169

Ex. 169

And Example 170 proves that all rules were meant to be challenged. First, the details: Lock onto high *D* at the fifteenth fret with a reinforced third finger for the opening *E* bends in bar 1. This stations your index finger at the thirteenth fret, your second finger at the fourteenth fret, and your pinky at the fifteenth fret to cover the remaining notes in the measure. Drop down the neck, then slide back up into a prepared minor-third shape (remember this one?) to accommodate the tenth-position IV-chord lick in bar 2. Now, let's break some rules! While we've been stressing the fact that *G#* is a touchy tone to deal with in an *A* blues and is best suited for use with the V chord, the *G#* in bar 1 would *not* affect its substitution as a I- or IV-chord lick because it is played as a passing tone and falls on a weak beat. So go ahead and drop this one anywhere you wish. Also, the "forbidden" *C#* works over *D7* in bar 2 because it anticipates the upcoming *A7* in bar 11 of the progression, which makes this as fine a I or IV lick as any.

Track 170

Ex. 170

TURNAROUNDS

Why fourteen turnarounds? We here at *Blues Lick Factory* have long maintained the notion that you can learn a lot about blues guitarists by listening to their turnarounds. This final two-bar segment of the 12-bar blues progression—bars 11 and 12, to be precise—seems to serve as a musical watering hole of sorts, a place where players often return to their favorite pet licks while they nourish and gather their thoughts before launching another 12-bar chorus. Turnarounds also tend to make great intros, endings, and can often be dropped into any part of a 12-bar progression. To create an ending from any of the following turnarounds, put a chromatic neighbor ♭II7 chord (*Bb7*) or VII7 chord (*G#7*) on the downbeat of beat *two* in bar two and follow it with a tonic *A7* on the third eighth note of the same beat, holding, or tremoloing, the I chord until a cued cutoff.

We'll begin with a half-dozen single-note turnarounds. In this reworking of the one-bar I-chord lick in Example 119a, Example 171 decorates a simple repetitive *A* root and then a descending *A* blues-scale run with grace-note hammer-ons and slurs before wrapping up with a chromatic climb to the root of *E7* in bar 2. You can alter the *Eb* grace note to *E* in this lick, which, by the way, also makes a great intro.

Track 171

Ex. 171

In Example 172, we again break the rules with taste and finesse by injecting *G#* as a chromatic passing tone between the ♭7 (*G*) and root (*A*). You may recognize beats *three* and *four* in bar 1 as a half-timed version of a previous six-note lick module from way back when, albeit in a different octave. A rhythmic variation of the previous chromatic climb to *E* concludes the chorus.

Track 172

Ex. 172

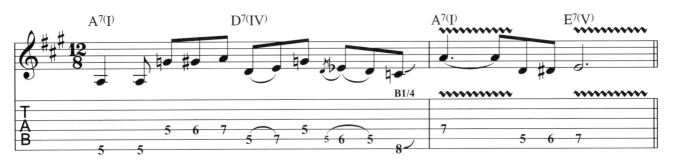

Example 173 combines elements of the two previous chromatic moves on beats *two* and *three* in bar 1, then inserts a slurred 4–♭5–4–♭3 (*D–Eb–D–C*) move—try bending this one—leading back to a hammered tonic *A* for the familiar conclusion in bar 2.

Track 173

Ex. 173

Example 174 shows how even the most common "lick module" can be turned into an effective turnaround. For a twist, try replacing the *A*'s in beats *two* and *three* of bar 1 with *G*'s or repetitive *E*'s. The three grace-hammered *C#*'s in bar 2 lock with the I chord before targeting the root of *E7* on beat *three*.

Track 174

Ex. 174

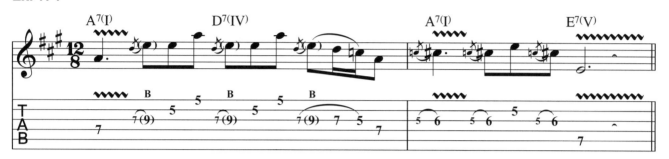

Example 175 nails the root of each chord change—*A7–D7–A7–E7*—on beats *one* and *three* in both measures. Begin in fifth position, then slide into the *F#* using your second finger to align your fretting hand in the tenth position for the next two beats as you cross over into bar 2. Finally, drop a whole step to the eighth position to exploit the *G–E* move and hook up with the V chord.

Track 175

Ex. 175

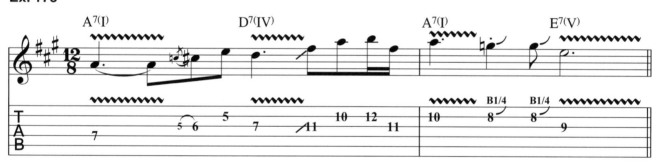

Following a third-finger slide into the root, the second two beats in bar 1 of Example 176 are appropriated from the I-chord lick in Example 161. And while the last four notes spell out a permuted *A7* arpeggio, the final *G* serves as a sassy *#9* over the V chord. A perfect match.

Track 176

Ex. 176

Each triplet on the last three beats of bar 1 in Example 177 surrounds a high pedal *A* with chromatically descending *G*'s, *Gb*'s, and *F*'s to create the illusion of partial chords in this turnaround. If you analyze it further, you'll discover that this combination of notes actually outlines key chord tones of *A7*, *D*, and *Dm*. The descending chromatic line comes to a rest on *E*, while the remaining snippet paraphrases Willie Dixon's classic "Hoochie Coochie Man" riff, albeit rhythmically displaced.

Track 177

Ex. 177

Example 178 features a chromatic descent and *A* pedal tone similar to those in the previous example, except here the points of departure and arrival are *E* and *A*, not *G* and *E*. The target is a partial *A* chord on the downbeat of bar 2. Realign your fret hand in the second position to grab the opening *A* with your first finger and the fifth-fret octave with your pinky. Playing the *E* on beat *two* with the third finger is recommended, as is following through with the second and first fingers on *Eb* and *D*, then shifting the first finger down to *C#*, but you should use whatever fingering feels most comfortable.

Track 178

Ex. 178

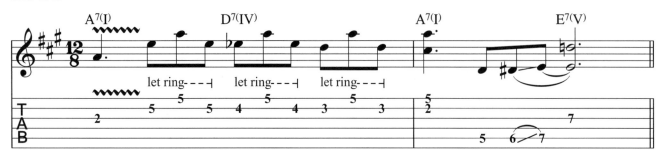

Example 179 reverses the strategy from Example 178. We begin with a chromatic climb up the *B* string from *C#* to *E*, alternating with the same pedal *A* and targeting a double-stopper five-root diad on the downbeat of bar 2. Sustain the *E* beneath the final *D* to create a partial *E7* chord.

Track 179

Ex. 179

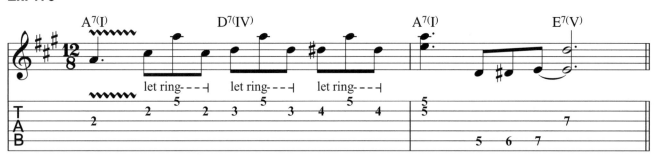

Example 180 digs back into Example 161, a seemingly popular well of source material. This time we're sliding the prefingered ♭7 over 5 (*G* over *E*) broken, or melodic, minor third intervals down in half steps—*G* over *E*, *G♭* over *E♭*, and *F* over *D*—en route to a grace-hammered *C#* target. Slide upward into the first prefingered minor third interval, then maintain or release pressure on both strings to control the desired amount of ring-over between notes as you move them chromatically downward. And yep, you guessed it: you can do the same move in reverse.

Track 180

Ex. 180

Example 181 takes the closely voiced arpeggiated intervals from Example 177 and recasts them as wide harmonic intervals, meaning both notes are played at the same time by lowering the descending notes one octave. The rhythm has also changed from eighth notes to a loping quarter–eighth-note shuffle.

Track 181

Ex. 181

In Example 182, we simply restore the eighth-note triplet feel and arpeggiate the harmonic intervals from the previous example. A certain little old band from Texas even turned this classic turnaround into a heavy, repetitive signature riff in more than one song.

Track 182

Ex. 182

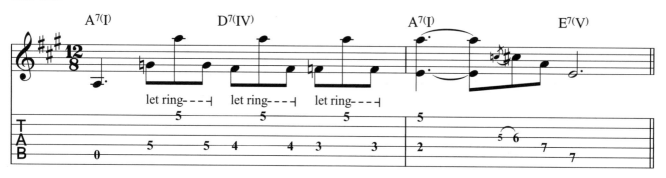

Example 183 brings a third note into the mix. This added chromatic run down the B string forms a string of chromatic major sixth intervals on the D and B strings that descend beneath our consistent A pedal tone.

Track 183

Ex. 183

We'll close out this roundup of turnarounds with Example 184, a direct descendant of Example 183, in which we split the descending major sixth intervals and pedal A's and incorporate a new dotted-eighth-sixteenth-eighth rhythmic scheme.

Track 184

Ex. 184

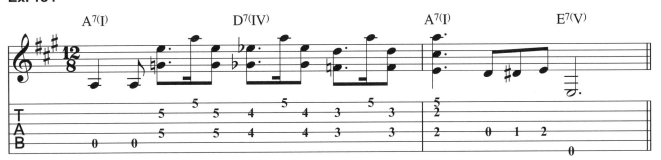

Get the idea? Now it's time to take the reins and formulate your own two-, four-, and eight-bar excursions and, ultimately, entire 12-bar blues solos. Think "call-and-response" phrasing, incorporate all of the licks, rhythmic variations, and other techniques you've acquired thus far, and just go for it. The upcoming trio of 12-bar solos will point you in the right direction.

CHAPTER 11

12-BAR BLUES SOLOS

Here comes the full Monty: an entire nonstop solo chorus—that's hep talk for one full cycle of a 12-bar blues progression. Actually, you get three complete choruses notated in a variety of 12/8 tempos. The first and third solos are played over quick-change progressions, while the second one cruises over a slow-change progression. Each solo sports a radically different approach.

On the disc: Each 12-bar solo gets its own audio track. Get ready to wail.

GUITAR SOLO #1

To demonstrate the flexibility of our pickup lick modules (and just to prove that it could be done), the first solo (Example 185) is an experimental exercise constructed from our first thirteen three-note pickup licks played in their order of appearance (see Examples 1a-c through 13a-c), plus a selection of choice target tones. Each 3/8 triplet in this moderately slow blues is played on beat *four* and simply serves as a one-beat pickup into a target tone on the downbeat, or beat *one*, of the following measure of 12/8. Of course, you wouldn't stick to such a repetitious rhythmic scheme in most real-life applications, so this may seem silly at first, but listen; you can hear the chord changes in these lazy lines, right? Point made. (Tip: Give each pickup lick a rhythm and phrasing makeover in order to improve its potential for success in the real world.)

Track 185

Ex. 185

Blues Solo #1

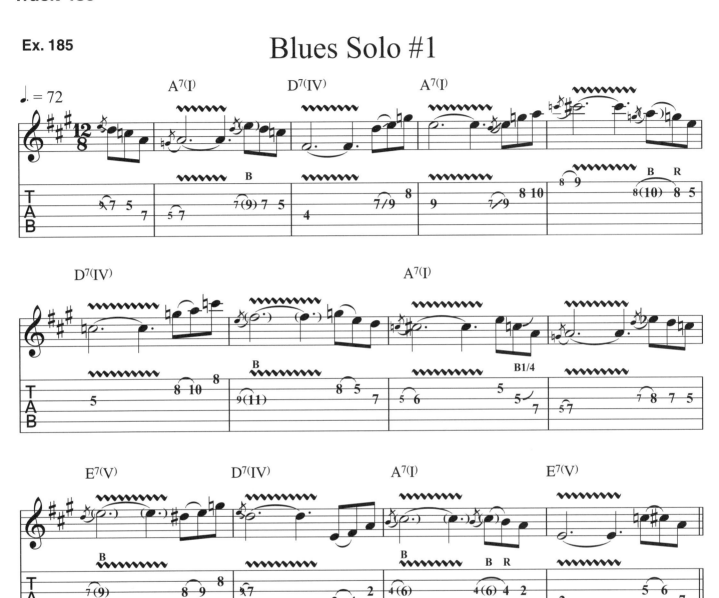

GUITAR SOLO #2

Keeping it simple and aggressive (think blues harp) is the name of the game for our next 12-bar solo in Example 186. This medium-tempo shuffle features an assortment of go-for-the-throat one-bar ostinatos, each one comprised of a single broken minor-third interval that we've used elsewhere. (Tip: You can also play these minor-third shapes, which make ideal landmarks for locating pentatonic scale patterns, as harmonic intervals.) Memorize their fret positions and how they react to each chord, and file this info for future reference.

Track 186

Ex. 186

GUITAR SOLO #3

Are we having fun yet? Okay, it's time to get serious. Our third and final solo (Example 187) digs deep into the garden of knowledge we've been growing and nurturing to formulate a sweet 'n' meaty 12-bar slow-blues excursion that uses almost every trick in the book. (Okay, in *this* book.) We begin with a three-note pickup into a one-bar motif that targets C#, the 3 of the I chord. The first three beats of this measure are adapted to the D7 chord in bar 2 simply by reducing the bent C# 's by one half-step to C, the ♭7 of the IV chord. Bar 3 reverses back to the A pentatonic major tonality of bar 1, but injects some breathing space in anticipation of the busy repetitive triplet motif that follows in bar 4. Once again, and this time in mid-lick, C# is adjusted to C—this time garnished with a saucy quarter-tone bend—to cover the next D7 change in bar 5. Note how the straight eighth-note triplets morph into lopsided dotted-eighth-sixteenth-eighth groupings on beats *three* and *four*. Continuing the emphasis on C into bar 6, we drop into the mid-register fifth-position A pentatonic blues box to navigate the return to the A7 in bar 7. This I-chord motif again targets C# and contains the time-honored unison slide to the tonic A on beat *three*, a move reminiscent of the "false fingering" technique employed by saxophonists. (And check out that tasty G# passing tone used to cross the bar line.)We repeat this motif in bar 8, but remain in eighth position for a three-note chromatic ascent (C–C#–D) that targets the bent V-chord root on the down-beat of bar 9. Following suit, we target the root of D7 on beat *one* of bar 10, but this time we head back to the fifth position for a measure of riffery that includes Eb, another touchy IV-chord no-no that nevertheless works in this case. A simple half-step move-ment from D to C# creates a momentary melodic suspension and provides the gateway to the turnaround in bars 11 and 12. (You can trace this one back to Example 175.) Take it and run with it because guess what? The next chorus is all yours.

Track 187

Ex. 187

Blues Solo #3

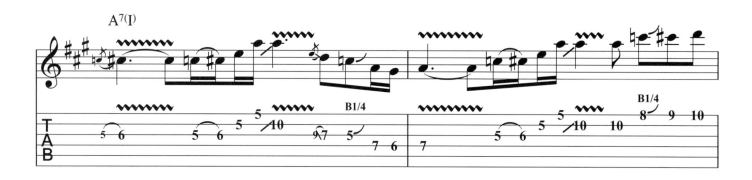

CHAPTER 12

ONE-BAR BLUES OSTINATOS

We've seen how the common chord tones and extensions in the I, IV, and V (*A7*, *D7*, and *E7*) chords allow many blues licks to be functional throughout an entire 12-bar blues progression, and it occurs to me that perhaps this book has neglected to stress the importance of repetition in blues music, so let's combine both concepts. Since so many of our licks work with all three chords, it's possible and often highly effective to "ride," or repeat, a single lick through an entire 12-bar progression, quick-change or slow-change. It's all about building tension and anticipation through sheer momentum. These "blues ostinatos," renamed after the classical term for this type of repetitive melodic pattern, also provide a great way to study how a given lick behaves over each chord. They can comprise a single beat, an entire measure, two bars, or even four bars. Here are fourteen one-bar blues ostinatos to get you started. Each measure consists of a one-beat lick played four times, then repeated. Play each one-bar example twelve times to cover one full 12-bar cycle. Get to know them well, and you'll soon realize that this concept can be applied to hundreds of licks. (Tip: Tempo-wise, be aware that many of these examples are more potent in moderately fast shuffles than extremely slow blues, where they run the risk of becoming interminable.)

On the disc: Each one-bar example is demonstrated twice following an initial four-beat countoff. For Examples 188a-b through 190a-b, each "a" and "b" example has been combined on one track with the "b" segment separated by an additional four-beat countoff. Examples 191a through 191h have been combined on a single track and are played nonstop with each segment preceded by a four-beat countoff.

Keeping it simple is often the best tack, and it doesn't get much more basic than the repetitive, double-stopped root-over-5 eighth-note triplets in Example 188a and gradually quarter-bent dotted-quarter tritones in Example 188b. (Tip: Try subbing harmonic minor-third intervals comprised of *G* over *E*, *A* over *F#*, or *C* over *A*, which you can pick up from the 12-bar solo in Example 185, for the *A* over *E* in Example 188a.)

Track 188

Ex. 188a   Ex. 188b

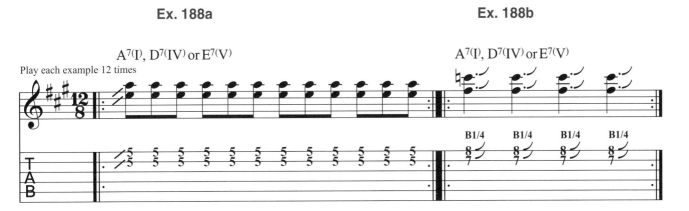

Examples 189a and 189b show off a pair of hotshot, fifth-position *A* blues box moves that can be easily tweaked to produce equally stimulating variations. (Tip: Try replacing the *E* in Example 189a with a first string/eighth fret *C#*, or simply with another *A*. Similarly, you can substitute *G* or an additional *E* for the *A*'s in Example 189b.)

Track 189

Ex. 189a   Ex. 189b

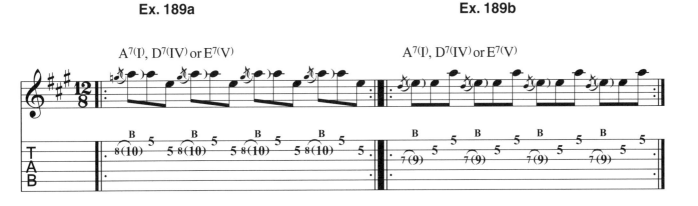

Our previous *A*-over-*E* double stops are embellished with grace-hammered *F#*'s in Example 190a, while a simple rhythmic variation adds a twist and additional motion to the second half of Example 190b. (Tip: Be careful. These moves are so comfy that you may be tempted to ride them through two or more choruses.)

Track 190

Ex. 190a   Ex. 190b

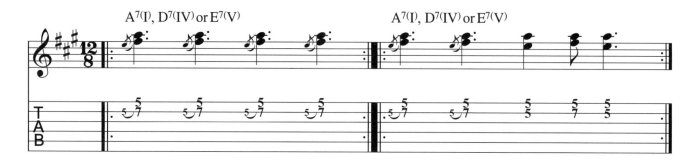

The next eight-part example (Example 191a–h) illustrates how to build a blues ostinato from each note in the *A* blues scale, plus the 2/9 (*B*) and 6/13 (*F#*) on loan from *A* pentatonic major. Here's the rundown: Example 191a begins on *A*; Example 191b begins on *B*; Example 191c begins on *C*; Example 191d begins on *D*; Example 191e begins on *E♭*; Example 191f begins on *E*; Example 191g begins on *F#*; Example 191h begins on *G*. (Tip: Journey beyond the ostinato and play Example 191a through 191h in sequential order for one bar each to create an exciting and impressive ascending pentatonic/blues sequence. Reduce each lick to half a measure to up the excitement ante.)

Track 191

(Parting Tip: It's cool to whip out these flashy tension builders and attention getters, as long as you know when to stop!)

CHAPTER 13

ONE-BAR BLUES RHYTHM FIGURES

The following dozen low-register single-note riffs make great blues rhythm figures, especially when you double them with a bass. All of these multipart examples are presented as I (*A7*) chord figures, but every one is easily movable to the IV (*D7*) and V (*E7*) chords in the same manner that tritones and chord shapes are transposed, so they can be used to create complete 12-bar slow-change or quick-change blues accompaniments. Here's the skinny: Raise each I-chord figure two and one-half steps (five frets) to cover the IV chord and three and one-half steps (seven frets above the I-chord riff, or two frets higher than the IV-chord figure) to cover the V. Keep track of the roots, memorize their fretboard shape, and apply them to any key. You can also start the I-chord riff on the next higher adjacent string at the same fret position for the IV chord, and either a whole step higher than that, or at the same fret position on the next lower adjacent string for the V chord. Once you become familiar with these transpositions, use these rhythm figures to record your own 12-bar blues backing tracks. (Or discover buried treasure in the bonus 12-bar rhythm tracks located at the end of the disc.)

The beauty of these movable rhythm figures is that they can multitask until the cows come home. Play 'em slow for slow blues, or speed 'em up for medium and up-tempo shuffles. Play 'em with a swing eighth-note feel as written, or adapt 'em to a straight-eighth-and-sixteenth feel—the crying sky's the limit! (Tip: Try playing each example in open position; start on the open *A* string for the I chord, then switch to the open *D* and low *E* strings to cover the IV- and V-changes.) Here's a short, descriptive play-by-play to guide you through each example:

On the disc: Four lettered examples appear per track. Each I (*A7*) chord–based rhythm figure is preceded by a four-beat countoff, then played four times.

SINGLE-NOTE RHYTHM FIGURES

Example 192a kicks off the proceedings with a simple but groovin' root-octave-♭7–5 figure that makes a great candidate for transposition to the IV and V chords.

Example 192b is the same riff with a chromatic 4–#4/♭5–5 (*D–D#/E♭–E*) climb added on beat *four*. (Tip: Try alternating measures of 192a and 192b to create a two-bar rhythm figure.)

Example 192c introduces a bit of rhythmic syncopation and space using the same initial root–octave-♭7 motion with an octave, ♭7 and 5 (*A, G,* and *E*) move on beat *four*.

Example 192d changes up the first three beats, but features the same chromatic climb from Example 192b on beat *four*. (Tip: Try alternating measures of 192c and 192d to create a two-bar rhythm figure.)

Track 192

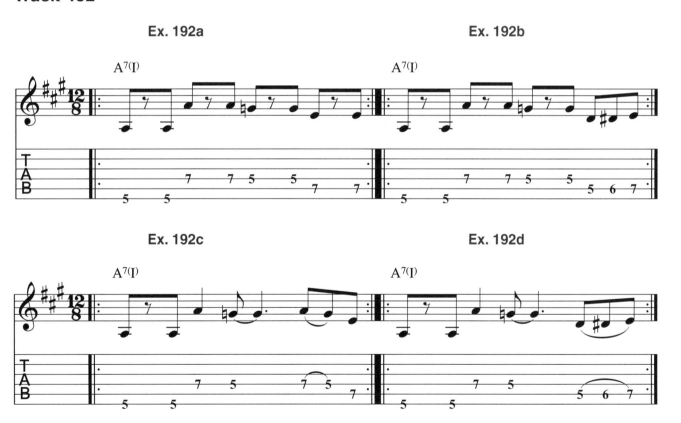

131

Example 193a introduces a cool, ascending root–3–5–♭7 (*A–C#–E–G*) riff, a simple *A* arpeggio if you think about it, then concludes with a descending octave/root–♭7–5 triplet (*A–G–E*). The slide into the 3 and ♭7–5 pull-off are critical phrasing elements in this riff.

Example 193b features a root–♭3—root–octave followed by the same closing triplet from Example 193a, albeit fingered and phrased in an entirely different manner. There's a bit of Howlin' Wolf's classic "Little Red Rooster" vibe and a little "Mercury Blues" lurking in the there.

Example 193c begins with a double root, then adds the ♭3, 3, a double 5, the 6, and another 5, all played with alternating quarter and eighth notes for a trademark Texas-shuffle groove.

Example 193d is the same riff with an octave *A* substituted for the final *E*. (Tip: Try alternating measures of 193c and 193d to create a two-bar rhythm figure.)

Track 193

Example 194a comes off like "Killing Floor" set to a shuffle beat. You can extract its classic riff from this double-root–double-3–triple-4–#4/♭5–5 figure by converting it to eighth and sixteenth notes (you'll need to add one extra on beat *three*) and playing it over a straight-eighth groove.

Example 194b's double-roots, 3's, and 5's, followed by the 6, octave/root, and 6, form a hybrid of Examples 194a, 193c, and 193d.

Example 194c features a double-root, ♭3–3–5 triplet, double-♭7, 6, and 5 in a decidedly British-sounding figure.

Example 194d is the same riff with a two-note variation on beat *four*. (Tip: Try alternating measures of 194c and 194d to create a two-bar rhythm figure.)

Track 194

CHORDAL RHYTHM FIGURES

Of course there are a million ways to comp chords in a standard 12-bar blues progression—that's another subject for another Lick Factory—but tempo, groove, and style are all contributing factors when it comes to creating solid chordal rhythm figures. The following dozen brief I-chord moves, many of which utilize partial chord shapes and function as counterpoint lines, will at least get you started. Transpose them to their IV- and V-chord positions—up two and one-half steps for *D7* and up three and one-half steps for *E7*—and run them through any 12-bar progression of your choice. (Tip: Try incorporating some of the tritone and seventh-chord voicings from Figures G through M into similar figures of your own design and transpose them to as many keys as possible.)

Each of the first four chordal rhythm figures builds on the previous one. Example 195a shows the time-honored alternating root plus 5–root plus 6 rhythm riff that jives with everything from "Red House" and "Hideaway"–style medium-tempo shuffles to half of Chuck Berry's catalog.

Example 195b throws this pattern slightly off-kilter by adjusting beats *two* and *four* to include only one partial root/6 chord. Though these two figures are nearly identical, it's best to stick to one or the other rather than alternating measures of each, as we did with several single-note rhythm riffs.

Example 195c extends Example 195a to include a root plus ♭7 diad on beat *three*. In this case, you may compile a two-bar pattern by alternating Example 195a with Example 195c, in that order.

Example 195d, which features the same ♭7 adjustment, is to Example 195c as Example 195b is to Example 195a. It makes sense in a Forest Gump kind of way.

Track 195

While the previous four examples work well at any tempo, the next four are best suited for slow, smoky blues grooves. Example 196a consists of a simple *A7* tritone played for a full beat and as a staccato eighth on beats *one* and *two*, then re-approached via slide from its lower chromatic neighbor (*G#7*).

Example 196b follows suit with four-note *A7* and *G#7* voicings.

Example 196c features a sustained *A7* tritone followed by two slick sliding sixth intervals (another tongue twister) that outline *A6* to *A9*.

Example 196d is to Example 196c as Example 196b is to Example 196a—almost. (Hey, it worked once.) Actually, the only difference besides the four-note seventh-chord voicings is the second staccato hit on beat *two*—the remaining notes in both figure are indeed identical.

Track 196

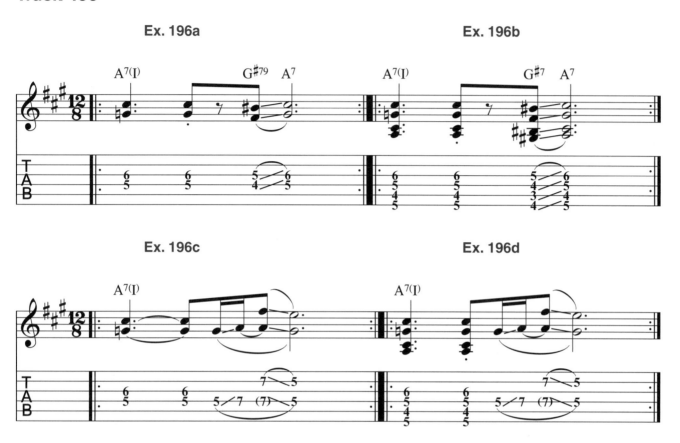

Ex. 196a Ex. 196b

Ex. 196c Ex. 196d

Example 197a continues the pilfering of materials from the last two examples with a one-beat *A7* tritone and some familiar slidin' sixths, which now begin with a milk chocolaty grace slide into beat *two* and surround a gooey, chromatic passing tone center.

In Examples 17a and 197b, we sub a four-note *A7* voicing for the previous tritone and tweak the rhythm of those island-approved sliding sixths.

Example 197c, a syncopated rhythm figure ideal for medium shuffles and up-tempo jump blues progressions, begins with a familiar *A7* chord before introducing a pair of sweet, three-note *A6* and *A9* voicings, formed by adding a third note to our favorite major sixth intervals, on the first and last eighth notes in beat *two*.

Finally, Example 197d takes us home with a cool, oblique ♭3–3 trill. Play the single-note *A* on the third eighth note in beat *one*, hit the partial *D* double stop on beat *two*, then anticipate beat *three* by lowering it one whole step and trilling the third string a half step higher while sustaining the *E* note on the second string. (Final Tip: Repeat the double stops from beat *two* on beat *four*, but replace the trill on the second one with a single oblique grace-note hammer onto *C#*. That's all, folks!)

Track 197

That brings us to the end of the assembly line. If you've found your stint at the *Blues Lick Factory* to be beneficial to your head, hands, and heart, then we've done our job. Thanks for your patronage, and we hope that our methods will help you to take the art of manufacturing blues guitar licks to new and even greater heights.

BLUES LICK FACTORY

ON THE CD

Note: *The tuning reference track is on Track 198.*

THREE-NOTE PICKUP LICKS

Track 1: Ex. 1a–Ex. 1c
Track 2: Ex. 2a–Ex. 2c
Track 3: Ex. 3a–Ex. 3c
Track 4: Ex. 4a–Ex. 4c
Track 5: Ex. 5a–Ex. 5c
Track 6: Ex. 6a–Ex. 6c
Track 7: Ex. 7a–Ex. 7c
Track 8: Ex. 8a–Ex. 8c
Track 9: Ex. 9a–Ex. 9c
Track 10: Ex. 10a–Ex. 10c
Track 11: Ex. 11a–Ex. 11c
Track 12: Ex. 12a–Ex. 12c
Track 13: Ex. 13a–Ex. 13c
Track 14: Ex. 14a–Ex. 14c
Track 15: Ex. 15a–Ex. 15c
Track 16: Ex. 16a–Ex. 16c
Track 17: Ex. 17a–Ex. 17c
Track 18: Ex. 18a–Ex. 18c
Track 19: Ex. 19a–Ex. 19c
Track 20: Ex. 20a–Ex. 20c
Track 21: Ex. 21a–Ex. 21c
Track 22: Ex. 22a–Ex. 22c
Track 23: Ex. 23a–Ex. 23c
Track 24: Ex. 24a–Ex. 24c
Track 25: Ex. 25a–Ex. 25c
Track 26: Ex. 26a–Ex. 26c
Track 27: Ex. 27a–Ex. 27c
Track 28: Ex. 28a–Ex. 28c
Track 29: Ex. 29a–Ex. 29c
Track 30: Ex. 30a–Ex. 30c
Track 31: Ex. 31a–Ex. 31c
Track 32: Ex. 32a–Ex. 32c

FOUR-NOTE PICKUP LICKS

Track 33: Ex. 33a–Ex. 33c
Track 34: Ex. 34a–Ex. 34c
Track 35: Ex. 35a–Ex. 35c
Track 36: Ex. 36a–Ex. 36c
Track 37: Ex. 37a–Ex. 37c
Track 38: Ex. 38a–Ex. 38c
Track 39: Ex. 39a–Ex. 39c
Track 40: Ex. 40a–Ex. 40c
Track 41: Ex. 41a–Ex. 41c
Track 42: Ex. 42a–Ex. 42c
Track 43: Ex. 43a–Ex. 43c
Track 44: Ex. 44a–Ex. 44c
Track 45: Ex. 45a–Ex. 45c
Track 46: Ex. 46a–Ex. 46c
Track 47: Ex. 47a–Ex. 47c
Track 48: Ex. 48a–Ex. 48c
Track 49: Ex. 49a–Ex. 49c
Track 50: Ex. 50a–Ex. 50c
Track 51: Ex. 51a–Ex. 51c
Track 52: Ex. 52a–Ex. 52c
Track 53: Ex. 53a–Ex. 53c
Track 54: Ex. 54a–Ex. 54c
Track 55: Ex. 55a–Ex. 55c
Track 56: Ex. 56a–Ex. 56c
Track 57: Ex. 57a–Ex. 57c
Track 58: Ex. 58a–Ex. 58c

FIVE-NOTE PICKUP LICKS

Track 59: Ex. 59a–Ex. 59c
Track 60: Ex. 60a–Ex. 60c
Track 61: Ex. 61a–Ex. 61c
Track 62: Ex. 62a–Ex. 62c

Track 63: Ex. 63a–Ex. 63c
Track 64: Ex. 64a–Ex. 64c
Track 65: Ex. 65a–Ex. 65c
Track 66: Ex. 66a–Ex. 66c
Track 67: Ex. 67a–Ex. 67c
Track 68: Ex. 68a–Ex. 68c
Track 69: Ex. 69a–Ex. 69c
Track 70: Ex. 70a–Ex. 70c
Track 71: Ex. 71a–Ex. 71c
Track 72: Ex. 72a–Ex. 72c
Track 73: Ex. 73a–Ex. 73c
Track 74: Ex. 74a–Ex. 74c
Track 75: Ex. 75a–Ex. 75c
Track 76: Ex. 76a–Ex. 76c
Track 77: Ex. 77a–Ex. 77c
Track 78: Ex. 78a–Ex. 78c
Track 79: Ex. 79a–Ex. 79c
Track 80: Ex. 80a–Ex. 80c
Track 81: Ex. 81a–Ex. 81c
Track 82: Ex. 82a–Ex. 82c
Track 83: Ex. 83a–Ex. 83c
Track 84: Ex. 84a–Ex. 84c
Track 85: Ex. 85a–Ex. 85c
Track 86: Ex. 86a–Ex. 86c
Track 87: Ex. 87a–Ex. 87c
Track 88: Ex. 88a–Ex. 88c
Track 89: Ex. 89a–Ex. 89c

SIX-NOTE PICKUP LICKS
Track 90: Ex. 90a–Ex. 90c
Track 91: Ex. 91a–Ex. 91c
Track 92: Ex. 92a–Ex. 92c
Track 93: Ex. 93a–Ex. 93c
Track 94: Ex. 94a–Ex. 94c
Track 95: Ex. 95a–Ex. 95c
Track 96: Ex. 96a–Ex. 96c
Track 97: Ex. 97a–Ex. 97c
Track 98: Ex. 98a–Ex. 98c
Track 99: Ex. 99a–Ex. 99c
Track 100: Ex. 100a–Ex. 100c
Track 101: Ex. 101a–Ex. 101c
Track 102: Ex. 102a–Ex. 102c
Track 103: Ex. 103a–Ex. 103c
Track 104: Ex. 104a–Ex. 104c
Track 105: Ex. 105a–Ex. 105c
Track 106: Ex. 106a–Ex. 106c
Track 107: Ex. 107a–Ex. 107c
Track 108: Ex. 108a–Ex. 108c
Track 109: Ex. 109a–Ex. 109c

RHYTHMIC VARIATIONS
Track 110: Ex. 110a–Ex. 110j
Track 111: Ex. 111a–Ex. 111h
Track 112: Ex. 112a–Ex. 112k
Track 113: Ex. 113a–Ex. 113j
Track 114: Ex. 114a–Ex. 114h
Track 115: Ex. 115a–Ex. 115h
Track 116: Ex. 116a–Ex. 116i
Track 117: Ex. 117a–Ex. 117h
Track 118: Ex. 118a–Ex. 118h

ONE-BAR TARGET-TONE BLUES LICKS
Track 119: Ex. 119a–Ex.119b
Track 120: Ex. 120a–Ex. 120b
Track 121 Ex. 121a–Ex. 121b
Track 122 Ex. 122a–Ex. 122b
Track 123: Ex. 123a–Ex. 123b
Track 124: Ex. 124a–Ex. 124b
Track 125: Ex. 125a–Ex. 125b
Track 126: Ex. 126a–Ex. 126b
Track 127: Ex. 127a–Ex. 127b
Track 128: Ex. 128a–Ex. 128b
Track 129: Ex. 129a–Ex. 129b
Track 130: Ex. 130a–Ex. 130b
Track 131: Ex. 131a–Ex. 131b
Track 132: Ex. 132a–Ex. 132b
Track 133: Ex. 133a–Ex. 133b
Track 134: Ex. 134a–Ex. 134b
Track 135: Ex. 135a–Ex. 135b
Track 136: Ex. 136a–Ex. 136b
Track 137: Ex. 137a–Ex. 137b
Track 138: Ex. 138a–Ex. 138b
Track 139: Ex. 139a–Ex. 139b
Track 140: Ex. 140a–Ex. 140b
Track 141: Ex. 141a–Ex. 141b
Track 142: Ex. 142a–Ex. 142b
Track 143: Ex. 143a–Ex. 143b
Track 144: Ex. 144a–Ex. 144b
Track 145: Ex. 145a–Ex. 145b
Track 146: Ex. 146a–Ex. 146b
Track 147: Ex. 147a–Ex. 147b
Track 148: Ex. 148a–Ex. 148b
Track 149: Ex. 149a–Ex. 149b
Track 150: Ex. 150a–Ex. 150b
Track 151: Ex. 151a–Ex. 151b
Track 152: Ex. 152a–Ex. 152b
Track 153: Ex. 153a–Ex. 153b
Track 154: Ex. 154a–Ex. 154b
Track 155: Ex. 155a–Ex. 155b

Track 156: Ex. 156a–Ex. 156b
Track 157: Ex. 157a–Ex. 157b
Track 158: Ex. 158a–Ex. 158b
Track 159: Ex. 159a–Ex. 159b
Track 160: Ex. 160a–Ex. 160b

TWO-BAR BLUES LICKS
Track 161: Ex. 161
Track 162: Ex. 162
Track 163: Ex. 163
Track 164: Ex. 164
Track 165: Ex. 165
Track 166: Ex. 166
Track 167: Ex. 167
Track 168: Ex. 168
Track 169: Ex. 169
Track 170: Ex. 170
Track 171: Ex. 171
Track 172: Ex. 172
Track 173: Ex. 173
Track 174: Ex. 174
Track 175: Ex. 175
Track 176: Ex. 176
Track 177: Ex. 177
Track 178: Ex. 178
Track 179: Ex. 179
Track 180: Ex. 180
Track 181: Ex. 181
Track 182: Ex. 182
Track 183: Ex. 183
Track 184: Ex. 184

12-BAR BLUES SOLOS
Track 185: Ex. 185
Track 186: Ex. 186
Track 187: Ex. 187

ONE-BAR BLUES OSTINATOS
Track 188: Ex. 188a–Ex. 188b
Track 189: Ex. 189a–Ex. 189b
Track 190: Ex. 190a–Ex. 190b
Track 191: Ex. 191a–Ex. 191h

ONE-BAR BLUES RHYTHM FIGURES
Track 192: Ex. 192a–Ex. 192d
Track 193: Ex. 193a–Ex. 193d
Track 194: Ex. 194a–Ex. 194d
Track 195: Ex. 195a–Ex. 195d
Track 196: Ex. 196a–Ex. 196d

Track 197: Ex. 197a–Ex. 197d

TUNE-UP
Track 198

BONUS 12-BAR RHYTHM TRACKS
Tracks 199–210

The accompanying CD was produced, engineered, and performed by JG at Jesilu Music, Woodstock, NY. All licks were performed live and without a pick, using a 1965 Fender Stratocaster through Line 6's Guitar Port.

Music notation is by JG, using Sibelius 2 software.

Digital file conversions by Robert Frazza.